Acknowledgements

To those who watched these films with me: Ivan Roots (the first time round), and my wife (all the other times).

Hollywood
1930s

Hollywood 1930s

Jack Lodge

GALLERY BOOKS

This book was devised and produced by
Multimedia Publications (UK) Ltd.

Editor: Richard Rosenfeld
Assistant editor: Sydney Francis
Production: Arnon Orbach
Design: Michael Hodson Designs
Picture Research: Vivien Adelman

First published in the United States of America 1985 by Gallery
Books, an imprint of W.H. Smith Publishers Inc., 112 Madison
Avenue, New York, NY 10016

ISBN 0 8317 4521 5

Typeset by Letterspace Ltd.
Origination by Clifton Studios Ltd., London
Printed in Italy by Sagdos

Contents

This page: *Bela Lugosi and Carol Borland in **Mark of the Vampire** (1935).*

Endpapers: *Fred Astaire and Ginger Rogers: the most famous dancing partnership in movie history.*

Page 1: *Marlene Dietrich in seductive form in **Morocco** (1930).*

Pages 2-3: *A classic Busby Berkeley number from **Footlight Parade** (1933).*

The Hollywood Studios

Chapter 1

Hollywood movies of the thirties came in all styles and sizes, but the best of them – and some of the worst – share a common quality. They are filled with confidence, and a confidence that at times borders on audacity. There are two very different reasons for this paradox. The world that these movies were made in, and for, was a world much lacking in confidence, a world that was slowly recovering from the Depression at the beginning of the period, and was to move at its end into the threat of war and, although not yet in America, into war itself. The second reason lies in the nature of the medium. The sound film was only three years old in 1930, and it was not merely a silent film with spoken words replacing intertitles; it was a radically different art. By all the rules of art the movies of the early thirties should have been immature, tentative things, not the brash and arrogant delights that, in fact, they were.

The films were like this because the film-makers themselves lived in an enclosed society cut off from surrounding social problems. Also, most of them had learned their craft in the studio system of the twenties where the technical excellence of the Hollywood film had reached a triumphant peak by around 1927. The studio system flourished for a further two decades and its virtues, outweighing its faults, gave the movies of the period their distinctive look and feel.

The magnificent seven

In the thirties there were seven leading studios, known as the "majors". Three of them were giants: Metro-Goldwyn-Mayer, Paramount and Warner Brothers, to be joined in 1935 by a fourth, when the two-year-old firm of Twentieth Century merged with the twenty-year-old Fox company to form Twentieth Century-Fox. A little below the giants in prestige and glamour, but often rivaling, and from time to time surpassing them in quality, were Universal, RKO Radio, and Columbia. In a sense there was an eighth major – United Artists – but this company was now primarily a releasing outfit, with its most important films made by the independent studio of Samuel Goldwyn.

Since the major studios owned their own chains of theaters, they had to produce the right quality and quantity of films to keep their theaters profitably filled. That meant producing almost one film a week; a year's output of fifty. And because the double feature was, by the thirties, a fact of theater-going, around half those fifty films were what are now referred to as B-movies, cheaply and quickly made, designed to entertain until the "big" picture started, but enjoying practically the very same technical facilities as more expensive productions.

*Jean Harlow and Wallace Beery in MGM's star-packed **Dinner at Eight** (1933). As they prepare to dine, Beery has his mind on a big deal; Harlow has hers on lover Edmund Lowe, and Beery knows it all too well.*

Main picture: *Nils Asther and Barbara Stanwyck in Frank Capra's* **The Bitter Tea of General Yen** *(1933).*
Far top right: *Gary Cooper at Helen Hayes' deathbed in Frank Borzage's* **A Farewell to Arms** *(1932). A great stage actress, Hayes made a handful of films in the early thirties, also appearing so successfully on the stage that she became known as the "First Lady of the American Theatre".*

Far bottom right: *Marlene Dietrich in* **Morocco.** *The lighting, the glitter, the costume and décor are the hallmarks of director Josef· von Sternberg and Paramount at this period.*

Writers, directors, cameramen, editors and others learned their trade on these B-movies. However, because these company-owned theaters provided a guaranteed release, and because the income was largely dependent on the numbers each main film attracted, the major studios felt no need to play it safe with their Bs, and exercised slightly less tight control over them. Although many of these small films were run off the "production line", many others were unexpected off-beat delights. And nearly all the Bs were economical and fast. Pared down to 55-65 minutes, they had to be.

Supporting cast

One of the great strengths of thirties Hollywood was the quality of acting in big and small films alike. There were great stars, as great as in any period, but also rosters of supporting players, colorful character actors for the most part, whom the major studios had under contract. These actors might be in thirty or forty films in any given year. Audiences welcomed the familiar faces; film buffs could put names to them. You could watch a thirties movie and recognize every credited player, and usually another half dozen who weren't even credited. When the studio system withered and contract players were no longer hired, this kind of continuity became impossible. It would be hard to name five or six small-part actors today. Thirties fans could name two hundred. No film was so bad that it did not contain half a dozen perfectly executed cameos. If stars, or script, or direction let you down there was always Allen Jenkins or Herman Bing, Ward Bond or Irving Bacon, to put things right. And a thirties Hollywood movie without George Chandler was a rare event.

That certain style

Most of the big studios developed a distinctive style. MGM spent the most money, and it showed in their richly furnished sets and elaborate spectacles. They were rich, too, in star quality, with Greta Garbo and Clark Gable, William Powell and Myrna Loy, Jean Harlow, Norma Shearer and Robert Montgomery among them, and by the end of the period the young Judy Garland, too. Some of their great successes have not aged kindly – *Smilin' Through* (1932) and *Mutiny on the Bounty* (1935), for example – but their polished comedies, their comedy-thrillers and their musicals stand up as fresh as ever. MGM made few of the period's masterpieces – apart from Clarence Brown they lacked a great director – because there was a prevalent blandness and unwillingness to take chances, but no MGM film was ever careless or tatty, and those stars could always carry the day. They made some of the finest Bs, too, but with their substantial resources these films had a finish that compared with that of some of the other studios' As.

Paramount was the most sophisticated of the majors. Originally known as Famous Players-Lasky (Paramount itself was once a distribution company), it went back almost to the earliest days of West Coast production, and throughout the twenties led the field. In the thirties the Paramount "look" became famous. Dazzling, often fantastic sets, camerawork that seemed to have a peculiarly luminous quality and acting with a casual elegance all contributed to a string of visual successes. The main contributor was Paramount's art director Hans Dreier, who came to Paramount from German films in the twenties and had an enormous share in making films like *Trouble in Paradise*, *Love Me Tonight* (both 1932) and *The Devil Is a Woman* (1935). In its directors, too, Paramount was unequalled, with Ernst Lubitsch, Rouben Mamoulian, Josef von Sternberg and Mitchell Leisen all working mainly for that studio during the period.

Bottom left: *Henry Fonda and Bette Davis in William Wyler's* **Jezebel** *(1938). For her performance as a headstrong Southern beauty Davis won her second Academy Award as Best Actress: her first had been three years earlier, for* **Dangerous.** *In 1938 Fonda was still making his way. One year on he appeared in* **Young Mr Lincoln** *with John Ford, his stepping stone to stardom.*

Main picture: *Will Rogers in Henry King's **State Fair** (1933). King and John Ford between them brought the best out of Rogers, underlining his quiet sensitivity, and turning a homespun philosopher into a notable actor.*

Crime pays at Warners

The average Warner Brothers product hardly seemed to come from the same world. Warners concentrated on contemporary, often low-life material. They made the best crime and gangster films; for a short but glorious period around 1933 they produced the best musicals (still unrivaled), and they had a nice sideline in the macabre. They, too, had a great art director in Anton Grot, who could give the flavor of a German silent to a horror film as easily as he could create the shimmering magic of *A Midsummer Night's Dream* (1935). The volatile and enormously versatile Hungarian Michael Curtiz was the studio's leading director in the period, flitting from genre to genre and always giving his movies pace and a gutsy flavor, while the German William Dieterle could make a routine studio chore like *Fog Over Frisco* (1934) into an astounding display of calculated eccentricity.

Twentieth Century-Fox never quite reached the level of those three (they had started rather later, after all). That they are best remembered now, as far as the thirties go, for their Charlie Chan series of B-movie detection – admirable as the best of the Chans are – does not say a great deal for the overall quality of the studio's major movies. They made a lot of very creditable, very enjoyable pictures, but somehow the indefinable spark that might have transformed a good studio into a great one never quite ignited. There were some average musicals – made to seem better than they were by the charming Alice Faye – and there was Shirley Temple to bring in the cash. Late in the decade the great director Fritz Lang arrived, but for most of the thirties John Ford, who worked frequently at the studio throughout the period, was the only major talent of which the company could boast.

At the beginning of the thirties Columbia was scarcely rated as a major. Columbia's studios were in Gower Street – in the heart of Hollywood – a thoroughfare associated with the numerous minor and short-lived companies that worked there. Columbia took time to shake off these 'Poverty Row' connections, but with *It Happened One Night* in 1934 the studio managed it, and that picture gave them unarguable major status. The talent of director Frank Capra and the drive of studio chief Harry Cohn ensured that they kept it.

Far left: *Peter Lorre as Raskolnikov in Joseph von Sternberg's **Crime and Punishment** (1935). This was Lorre's second Hollywood film, and a prestige production reinforcing Columbia's claim to major status.*

Left: *John Boles and Margaret Sullavan in John M. Stahl's **Only Yesterday** (1933). This was Sullavan's first film, to which she brought a unique mixture of resolution and vulnerability.*

Perfect horrors

Universal made many pretty dire movies, their B-Westerns and B-musicals among them, but they also made the superb horror films that began with *Dracula* and *Frankenstein* (both 1931); they had one director in James Whale who for a few years could seemingly do no wrong, whether in horror movies, romantic comedies or sophisticated thrillers, and they could from time to time come up with something as shattering as the anti-war epic *All Quiet on the Western Front* (1930). You could forgive many a Universal disaster for the sake of that one extraordinary achievement.

And finally, RKO. This was the most totally unpredictable of the studios. RKO made so many offbeat and quirky movies that oddness sometimes seemed to be the studio's norm. Fortunately most of the oddness was entirely enjoyable, and a studio that from time to time came out with such widely different masterpieces as *King Kong* (1933), *The Informer* (1935), *Winterset* (1936), *Stage Door* (1937) and *Bringing up Baby* (1938) could easily be forgiven any lapses. There were also their Astaire-Rogers musicals and a fair quota of attractive Bs, although in that field RKO's golden days would come a little later with the Val Lewton unit. In short, RKO was the connoisseur's studio, and fifty years on it still looks just like that.

Outside the majors, there was Walt Disney, who ventured into feature-length movies with *Snow White and the Seven Dwarfs* (1938); from 1935 on there was Republic, making mainly action-filled Bs but destined for higher things in the forties; and a number of small and often short-lived outfits that were still capable of surprising everyone, as Tiffany did with James Whale's *Journey's End* in 1930, based on the play by R.C. Sheriff.

These then were the sources of our thirties pleasures. When the films are seen again today, remarkably few of them fail the test of time. The age looks an age of endless richness, an age when a great popular art engaged people with an intensity difficult to imagine now. For today there is art-house cinema on the one side, youth-orientated spectaculars on the other, and the great middle ground of movies for everyone lies almost empty. In the thirties it was full. There were no bad years in that decade, and two of the years, 1933 and 1939, seem beyond argument the sound cinema's greatest heights.

Right: *Miriam Hopkins surrounded by admirers in Rouben Mamoulian's* **Becky Sharp** *(1935). This was the first feature film to be made in the new three-color Technicolor process, and this particular scene was a dazzling success.*

Below: *Richard Carlson, Janet Gaynor and Minnie Dupree in* **The Young in Heart** *(1938). Gaynor plays one of a charming family of confidence tricksters who, under Dupree's benign influence, see the error of their ways. The film was a pleasant trifle; after it, Gaynor, who 10 years earlier had won the first ever Best Actress Oscar, retired.*

14

Crime and Punishment

Chapter 2

With the thirties the crime film became, for the first time, a major genre. It was there, of course, in the early days of cinema, but then, in films like D.W. Griffith's *The Musketeers of Pig Alley* (1912) and Thomas Ince's *The Gangsters and the Girl* (1914), crime had been seen more as a working-class aberration, engendered by poverty, than as the glamorous pursuit it later became. The romantic twenties, at least in their major films, preferred to leave crime on one side, although the gangster cycle had one distinguished forerunner in Josef von Sternberg's *Underworld* (1927), and the macabre creations through which Tod Browning guided Lon Chaney prefigured much that was to recur in crime and horror films when sound came.

Big-city blues

An outstanding year for the crime movie was 1931, when William A. Wellman made *The Public Enemy*, propelling James Cagney to stardom. This film, like the early silents, points its finger at the sadness and deprivation of the big city as the cause of crime. The mood is drab and low-key. Cagney, in only his second year in films, and cast originally as the hero's friend, made so dynamic an impression that Warner Brothers tried switching his role with that of Edward Woods, and Cagney seized his chance. That rapid delivery, pugnacious strut and penetrating glare carried the actor through thirty years of stardom.

In this film he plays a tough youngster tempted into petty crime, attaching himself to the local bigshots, and enjoying a brief year or two of luxury (during which he pushes the celebrated grapefruit into Mae Clarke's face) before, in one of cinema's most jolting scenes, he is kidnapped from a hospital bed and delivered, trussed up and swathed in bandages, at his mother's front door. Indeed, the film set a new standard of ruthlessness: when the gangster who is Cagney's boss dies from a fall from his horse, Cagney and his sidekick go to the stable with revolvers to execute the offending animal.

Warners had two other great successes in the crime field in 1931, both directed by Mervyn LeRoy. *Little Caesar* did for Edward G. Robinson what *The Public Enemy* did for Cagney. Cagney at his most vicious had a sympathetic side (his mother loved and admired him throughout *The Public Enemy*), but Robinson's Rico in *Little Caesar* is coarse, vain, flashy and utterly repellent. The film is quintessential thirties Warners – gray and unlovely, rancid and corrupt. There is no trace of sentiment or glamour. Robinson's gang boss has his days of power and wealth, then sinks to the flop-house and finally to a wretched and dismal death in a deserted street.

*A shocked Phillips Holmes reads of the discovery of Sylvia Sidney's body in Sternberg's **An American Tragedy** (1931). This was to have been directed by the great Russian director Sergei Eisenstein, but Paramount rejected his treatment of Dreiser's novel, and consequently withdrew their offer to him.*

843 -

Below: *James Cagney, Joan Blondell and Edward Woods in William A. Wellman's* **The Public Enemy** *(1931). The positions on the stairway are prophetic. The film sent Cagney to the top; Blondell flowered as a perky comedienne, but remained a star of middle rank; Woods was little heard of after this.*

Right: *Edward G. Robinson radiates a gloating defiance in* **Little Caesar** *(also 1931).*

In LeRoy's *Five Star Final* Robinson's image is softer than his later one. Here he is an unscrupulous newspaper editor who in the pursuit of increased sales decides to dig up an ancient scandal, and in so doing drives a decent man and wife to suicide. This time there is a final cop-out, with Robinson allowed to repent and change his ways, but until then it is harsh, unsparing drama, with some fine supporting playing, notably from Aline MacMahon as Robinson's adoring secretary and Boris Karloff (with *Frankenstein* and his own stardom a few months ahead) as an unctuous ex-clergyman chasing the dirt.

Killer's code

Still in 1931, Karloff is just as impressive in Howard Hawks' *The Criminal Code*, one of the first of the prison movies that became so popular in the first years of sound. Perhaps Hawks (who was to prove, alongside John Ford, the finest of thirties directors) had not quite come to terms with sound, for there is a certain tentativeness about the film, and a lack of Hawks' characteristic warmth and easy openness.

Nonetheless the film has its fine moments, most memorably in the scene in which Karloff, as a prisoner who is the warden's barber, uses the tool of his trade to despatch a squealer who has violated the code of the title.

Rouben Mamoulian's *City Streets* (1931) is a gangster film with a difference. It is a love story beautifully played by Sylvia Sidney and the young Gary Cooper, interwoven with bootlegging and murder. In his early movies Mamoulian was so in love with the medium and its innovatory possibilities that in this film, as in his next, the entrancing musical *Love Me Tonight* (1932), he uses a whole battery of technical experiments. *City Streets* has bravura camerawork, expressionist lighting, distorted sound, the odd touch of symbolism, but none of it is permitted to get in the way of an exciting story lucidly told. Mamoulian was also one of Broadway's most distinguished stage directors.

Rowland Brown's *Quick Millions* (1931) was the first of only three films that this talented director made. Brown did not take easily to the studio system which denied the director's right to the ultimate decision, and his directorial career allegedly ended when he punched a supervisor. (Thereafter he became a scriptwriter.) *Quick Millions*, made for Fox before the merger with Twentieth Century, shows what a talent was lost. The film stars Spencer Tracy, who back in the early thirties was far from the benign and friendly father-figure of his

Inset far left: *Edward G. Robinson with, on the receiving end, Douglas Fairbanks Jr (second from left), in* **Little Caesar** *(1931). Note the cat on the counter, framing the composition.*

Left: *Spencer Tracy and Marguerite Churchill in* **Quick Millions** *(1931). In this shot there seems to be a trace of the later, kindly Tracy, but it is very misleading. Early thirties Tracy was every bit as rough and tough as they come.*

Below: *Phillips Holmes and Walter Huston in Howard Hawks'* **The Criminal Code** *(1931).*

C-5-54

famous days. The younger Tracy often played a snarling tough, and in Brown's movie he is a truck-driver who rises to become a powerful racketeer. This is another fast and savage film, and its world accepts the murder of people as a casual fact of life.

One director, however, ended his career in 1931. Roland West had been directing on and off since 1918, and his best work had shown a flair for eerie atmospheres and a somewhat grisly humor. His 1925 Lon Chaney silent, *The Monster*, is a good example, being set in a sanatorium presided over by an insane doctor intent on resuscitating the dead. West's last two films (both 1931) were *The Bat Whispers*, a beguiling mixture of detective thriller and old-dark-house horror comedy, and *Corsair*, a more straightforward, vigorous thriller about rumrunners during Prohibition (which ended with Roosevelt's election the following year). West, a somewhat shadowy and mysterious character, never directed again, for reasons still unknown. Certainly those last films, especially *The Bat Whispers*, with its striking sets and restlessly prowling camera, show no lessening of his talents.

Shame of a nation

Next year, 1932, brought two of the greatest crime movies. One was Howard Hawks' *Scarface – Shame of a Nation*. Hawks had found himself with a vengeance. *Scarface* is as devoid of pity as any of those 1931 films, but it also brings to the gangster film a sardonic, biting humor that no other similar movie possesses. Essentially the same story as *Little Caesar*, the rise and fall of a gang boss, and based this time on the career of Al Capone, *Scarface* is an exuberant, bouncing film about a character whose larger-than-life vigor almost bursts out of the screen. Paul Muni is excellent as Tony Camonte, who revels in his power and his apparent immunity from the law.

This was just before the Breen code set sharply defined limits to what a film could say or show, and even in 1932 *Scarface* contains one interpolated scene in which a group of good citizens is shown making up their minds to do something about such lawlessness. But that is the only moment that rings false. Hawks used the moving

Left: *Issuing prison clothes to Spencer Tracy proves somewhat difficult. The film is* **Twenty Thousand Years in Sing Sing** *(1933), based on the memoirs of prison guard Lewis E. Lawes, and remade by Warners in 1940 as* **Castle on the Hudson/Years Without Days,** *with John Garfield in the Tracy role.*

Below and bottom: *Paul Muni as Tony Camonte and Ann Dvorak as his sister Cesca in Howard Hawks'* **Scarface** *(1932). Tony, jealous of any man's attentions to Cesca, has dragged her away from a dance, and a violent quarrel ensues.*

Top right: *Donald Woods, Margaret Lindsay, Bette Davis and Lyle Talbot in* **Fog Over Frisco** *(1934).*
Top left: *The perfect marriage: William Powell and Myrna Loy in* **After the Thin Man** *(1936).*
Above *Paul Muni in* **I am a Fugitive from a Chain Gang** *(1932). This was such an effective movie that it was one of the few films to promote social reform, giving voice to and shaping the public's antagonism toward chain gangs.*

camera sparingly, but always to telling effect, and never more so than in the marvelous opening passage of *Scarface*, with the camera gliding through deserted rooms littered with the débris of a wild party, and the killer (Muni) stalking his victim. Memorable, too, is the killing of another rival (Karloff yet again), despatched in a bowling alley just after he has released his ball, with the camera following it into the pins, and the last pin tottering to fall with a sickening finality.

No hiding place

I am a Fugitive from a Chain Gang, directed in 1932 by Mervyn LeRoy, is a harrowing experience, based on the true story of Robert E. Burns, who was condemned to a Georgia chain gang for a small, unwitting part in a minor crime, escaped, made good, returned on a promise of parole, and was finally betrayed. The film follows its protagonist (Muni again) with an unflinching realism through to the hopeless end. Muni escapes a second time, and meets, for a moment, the girl who loves him (Helen Vinson). She asks how he lives. "I steal," he answers, quietly, and fades into the dark. LeRoy was a superb director of hard-hitting, socially aware movies, both in his handling of actors and in his creative use of sound, particularly in this film in the scenes on the chain gang.

The best crime movie of 1933 was another prison drama, Michael Curtiz's *Twenty Thousand Years in Sing Sing*, with Spencer Tracy, again in his tough guy persona, released on parole and going back of his own accord to confess to a crime committed by his girl. There is no escape here – Tracy goes to the chair. The girl is played with a fragile, nervous intensity by Bette Davis, who quarrelled a year or two later with the studio, Warner Brothers, because she was being cast in so many crime films and other undignified affairs. Time has played a wicked irony here, for the early Davis films like this one, *Three on a Match* (1932), *Bureau of Missing Persons* (1933), and *Fog Over Frisco* (1934), and her performances in them, look far better now than some of the lavish costume pictures and highly regarded sob stories of her later days.

The film historian William K. Everson called *Fog Over Frisco*, directed by William Dieterle, the fastest film ever made, and that verdict still stands. Dieterle races his characters upstairs and downstairs, in and out of cars and ships, into nightclubs and out in a couple of minutes, and manages to wrap up an intrigue of bewildering complexity in barely an hour. Davis is the bad girl, Margaret Lindsay (Warners' ever-charming girl-next-door) the good one, and nothing about the movie is normal. The star (Davis) is the victim, murdered half way through, Douglas Dumbrille for once is *not* the killer and the good girl's name is Val, which isn't short for Valerie but believe it or not Valkyr!

Opposite page: *William Powell as Nick Charles, amateur detective, seeking inspiration from a fictional colleague. This is a scene from* **The Thin Man Goes Home** *(1944). The series lasted into the forties.*

Right: *This was a vital letter, until terrier Asta got to work – from the first* **Thin Man** *(1934). Unlike some movie dogs, Asta never played leads, but this engaging hound deserved to. He triumphed again in* **Bringing Up Baby** *(1938).*

Below: *Spencer Tracy and the stray which has attached itself to him in jail in Fritz Lang's* **Fury** *(1936).*

Enter the Thin Man

In 1934 the comedy murder mystery cycle began with MGM's *The Thin Man*. This film has everything going for it: a superb plot (courtesy of Dashiell Hammett), whiplash direction from 'One-take Woody' Van Dyke, the first appearance of the terrier Asta (the best canine actor since the great Rin-Tin-Tin), lots of MGM gloss, and above all the pairing of William Powell and Myrna Loy as amateur sleuth Nick Charles and his wife Nora. Loy, after years playing dubious oriental ladies and the like, blossomed as an enchanting comedienne, and teamed beautifully with the dry and quizzical Powell. They fill the screen with the easy badinage of a happy marriage.

There were to be five more "Thin Man" films, all with Powell and Loy (the last in 1947), and if they did tail off a little towards the end, they added up to one of the period's most reliable pleasures. Murder-cum-comedy, usually with husband-and-wife teams, caught on. RKO's *The Ex-Mrs Bradford* (1936) had Powell opposite the delectable Jean Arthur, and was virtually another "Thin Man" film, and MGM themselves brought out three nice little programmers (not quite As and not quite Bs) in the "Fast Company" series, with a married couple doing the detecting in the pleasantly original surroundings of the rare book business. Universal, too, joined in the act with *Remember Last Night?* (1934), with director James Whale showing himself as much at home with a rapid-fire mystery in a heavy-drinking socialite milieu as he had been in the World War I trenches or the austere castle of Victor Frankenstein.

War on crime

By 1935 the Breen code was in full operation, and the impact on the gangster film was noteworthy. There were two important gangster films that year, and each of them in its different way showed that the moral climate had changed. Cagney could no longer play a killer and still carry the audience's sympathy: in Warners' *G-Men*, directed by William Keighley, a friend's death results in his joining the FBI – the war against crime is conducted with a heavy emphasis on law and order. *G-Men* had its exciting moments, and Cagney was never a dull actor, but some of the pre-Breen flavor had gone.

John Ford's *The Whole Town's Talking* (also 1935) adopts different tactics. Edward G. Robinson still plays a vicious thug, but to make it abundantly clear that he is no longer the hero, he also plays the role of the thug's double, an innocuous clerk who is constantly mistaken for him. This was much the better picture of the two. Jean Arthur as the clerk's girlfriend joyously seizes her chance to pose as a gun-moll; one of the great character actors, bald, bewildered Donald Meek, has one of his richest parts as a little man desperately trying to get the reward for spotting the killer. Although it tends to be forgotten, Ford in his middle period handled comedy with splendid panache (as in *Steamboat Round the Bend* the same year). *The Whole Town's Talking* may have the thinnest of plots, but for those players and that director it was quite enough.

Exiled from Nazi Germany, the great director Fritz Lang went to MGM for his first American film, *Fury* (1936). At first the studio thought little of the film, but it became an enormous critical success, and Lang's American career, which was to be as remarkable as his previous one in silent and sound films in Germany, was assured. The hero of *Fury* (Spencer Tracy, here playing an ordinary nice guy) is a man wrongfully accused of kidnapping, and narrowly escapes being lynched by a small-town mob. Believed dead, he hides out while a zealous DA prosecutes his attackers for murder until conscience sends him back to town. Lang gave the film a throbbing urgency, moving from the tenderness of the opening scenes between Tracy and his girl (Sylvia Sidney) to the appalling frenzy of the attack upon the prison in which Tracy is detained, and then to a superb court-room scene in which newsreel film of the attack is played to confound the defendants' well-planned alibis.

Bogart in town

Archie Mayo's *The Petrified Forest* (1936) brought Humphrey Bogart back to the screen. Bogart had made a few unimpressive appearances (usually in minor films) a few years before, and had returned to the stage. There he played a killer on the run, Duke Mantee, in Robert E. Sherwood's *The Petrified Forest*, and he repeated the role when Warners filmed the play. Highly praised at the time, the film now seems overstrained and whimsical, with Leslie Howard and Bette Davis struggling with unconvincing parts as poet and waitress meeting in a gas-station in Arizona, but there is no mistaking Bogart's power. The sympathetic edge that he later gave to all his characters, however deplorable they were, is not yet here; his Mantee is little more than a savage animal, yet in him, somewhere, are the faintly discernible outlines of the later presence.

That presence is clearly recognizable in *Black Legion* (1937), also directed by Mayo. This is one of the most courageous, and most unjustly forgotten, films of the period. An overtly political movie, a rare event in thirties Hollywood, it casts Bogart as a factory worker who is passed over for a coveted foremanship in favor of a foreigner. Embittered by this, he joins a right-wing, "America first" organization, closely modeled on the Ku Klux Klan. Eventually, when he sees the iniquity of his new friends it is too late – his life is already destroyed. He is too deeply implicated in crime. There are few believable working-man heroes in Hollywood movies of the time. Bogart's portrayal here, rough, well-meaning, hopelessly confused, is one that demands belief. But the film has other merits, particularly in its closing courtroom scenes, which carry a powerful denunciation of the Klan and other similarly oppressive and wicked societies.

A miscarriage of justice

Where *The Petrified Forest* strives in vain for poetry, *Winterset*, directed by Alfred Santell in 1936 from Maxwell Anderson's verse play, achieves it effortlessly. This magnificent film takes as its starting point the Sacco/Vanzetti case, and imagines that years later the son of an unjustly executed man comes to New York in search of the men really guilty of the killing. A marvelous screenplay by Anthony Veiller replaced Anderson's verse, or most of it, with finely wrought poetic prose, and substituted a happy ending for the original's bleak tragedy, yet miraculously sustained the spirit of the piece, and even suggested that this was the more logical and more moving resolution.

The action of *Winterset* takes place in a huddle of tenements by the East River, a perfectly achieved studio design, and contains probably the greatest set of performances of the whole period. RKO wisely used most of the Broadway cast, which ensured that the lines would be spoken as they deserved to be, and of this group of actors, most relatively new to cinema, Burgess Meredith as the hero Mio, Margo as the girl he meets on his quest, and Eduardo Ciannelli as the real killer Trock Estrella, went on to new careers in films.

Margo, who couldn't be blamed for shortening her name, which was Marie Marguerita Guadalupe Teresa Estela Bolado Castilla y O'Donnell, had in fact made a film or two before *Winterset*. She had attracted attention as the girl murdered by Claude Rains in Ben Hecht and Charles MacArthur's imaginatively eccentric *Crime Without*

Far left: Henry Fonda in Fritz Lang's **You Only Live Once** (1937). Hollywood hated to waste good footage so the brilliant bank robbery sequence from this movie turned up again in **Dillinger** (1945)!

Left: Joel McCrea and Humphrey Bogart in William Wyler's **Dead End** (also 1937). This shot conveys the solidity and detail of Richard Day's magnificent studio set, infinitely more effective than any location shooting could ever be. Bogart made seven films in 1937. In **Dead End** he played a vicious hoodlum. In **Marked Woman (below),** made earlier the same year, he was an idealistic District Attorney, here seen trying to persuade Bette Davis to help him nail the vice ring run by Eduardo Ciannelli. Davis' sister, played by Jane Bryan, is killed by the ring, so Davis talks, but not before she has been badly scarred by the gang.

Below: Bogart, in **Dead End** (1937), visiting his mother, superbly played by Marjorie Main. This was her first important film part at the comparatively late age of 47; she went on to specialize in comedy.

Inset below: Cagney and Bogart, this time in **Angels With Dirty Faces** (1938). The film ingeniously combines a social conscience with the crackling vitality of the gangster genre.

Below right: Cagney, in a scene from the same film, visited in jail by Bogart playing the crooked lawyer whom Cagney eventually kills.

Passion (1934), and later on played effectively in Frank Capra's *Lost Horizon* (1937). Meredith was a fine, sensitive actor whose rare thirties appearances were eagerly awaited. They include a piece of zestful comedy in another forgotten movie, S. Sylvan Simon's *Spring Madness* (1938), and an impressive part as the pacifist in Clarence Brown's *Idiot's Delight* (1939), in which the plot cruelly removed him after a couple of reels and left one with a hopelessly miscast Clark Gable and Norma Shearer for the rest of the long trek.

Ciannelli had no equal at depicting a quiet, sleek and lethal Latin, and he was again to feature in *Marked Woman* (1937). This was Bette Davis' last crime movie for Warners. It came after her quarrel with the studio, and represented something of a compromise. It was another crime melodrama. She plays a night-club hostess (it was impossible at that time to use a more accurate term) working under racketeers who scar her face savagely when she acts against their wishes. She gives the part her particular blend of bitterness and jaunty courage. The film, directed by Lloyd Bacon, was lavish, and admirably terse and pointed in its attack on corruption.

Criminal independents

In spite of the success of *Fury*, Fritz Lang and MGM parted after that film. Lang's second American effort, as uncompromising as the first, was *You Only Live Once*, which he made in 1937 for the independent producer Walter Wanger. Henry Fonda, just two years into his long career, plays a petty criminal whose ill luck and weakness lead to murder, a prison break and death. Cloaked in rain and mist, and heavy with the sense of destiny that had permeated Lang's German films, *You Only Live Once* has fittingly atmospheric photography from Leon Shamroy. It also has three fine performances: from Fonda himself; Sylvia Sidney, once again bravely ministering to a man in dire trouble; and, as the prison chaplain whom Fonda kills in his breakout, William Gargan, an underrated actor who was seldom as well served as here.

Another outstanding independent production of the time was *Dead End* (1937), directed by William Wyler for Samuel Goldwyn, and derived from Sidney Kingsley's hit Broadway play. Bogart plays a gangster returning to his old home in the riverside tenements of New York, with Joel McCrea and Sylvia Sidney as the architect and his girl caught up in the intrigue. In a film of superlative acting there are also the Dead End Kids – half a dozen streetwise youngsters who later appeared in *Angels With Dirty Faces* (1938).

Dead End's other fine performances came from Marjorie Main as Bogart's sad, harsh mother, and, best of all, Claire Trevor, one of the thirties' unsung talents, as the gangster's former sweetheart, now on the streets and ravaged by illness. The five minutes she was allowed contain the most memorable close-ups of the entire decade. The art director Richard Day also made a huge contribution to the movie, building an amazing cityscape of slum houses, waterfront, and rich men's towers which recalled the architectural splendors of the German silents. Day won seven Academy Awards, but curiously missed out with this, his finest work.

The rich year of 1937 also contained Mervyn LeRoy's *They Won't Forget*, perhaps the best of all Warners' crusading movies, and one of the thirties' finest in any genre. The film describes how a Southern court convicts, on the flimsiest of evidence, a Northern teacher of the murder of a schoolgirl (a very young Lana Turner), and how a Southern mob proceeds to lynch him. LeRoy's handling of the dangerous North-South hostility uses some striking visual coups,

Far left: *Former hoofer James Cagney's familiar glower, perfectly captured in this portrait by Hollywood photographer Scotty Welbourne, and his machine-gun delivery were turned to marvelous effect time after time by Warner Brothers during the thirties. Although Cagney was more accustomed to grappling with the likes of all-purpose Warners heavy Barton Maclane (**left**), in Lloyd Bacon's* **Frisco Kid** *(1935), he grappled, too, with molls like Jean Harlow (**above**), in William Wellman's* **Public Enemy** *(1931), the gangster film which shot him to immediate stardom.*

such as the moment when the lynching is conveyed by a shot of a speeding train snatching a mailbag from its container by the track. Claude Rains is superb as the self-seeking Southern lawyer, winning his case because he is a man of the people, which his Northern opponent, the smooth and cultivated Otto Kruger, so manifestly isn't. Allyn Joslyn as a cynical reporter, Clinton Rosemond as a terrified janitor who is going to be framed until a more profitable victim appears and Gloria Dickson as the teacher's wife all make *They Won't Forget* into one of the most fierce indictments of irrational emotional behavior. What one realizes only afterwards, when for a while the movie relinquishes its grip, is that the teacher might have been guilty after all. The script never reveals the guilty party.

Wild angels

Angels With Dirty Faces, directed by Michael Curtiz, shows Hollywood evading the demands of the Production Code in a highly ingenious way, but the duplicity was pardonable in view of the film's excitement and energy. Two slum kids dabble in juvenile crime. One of them (Pat O'Brien, settling down to a life of dependability after the flamboyant skulduggery of *The Front Page*, 1931) becomes the neighborhood priest, the other (James Cagney) becomes a cocky gangster idolized by the local youth (the Dead End Kids). When at the end Cagney is led to the chair, O'Brien, still his friend, persuades him to take the last walk as a babbling coward to break his influence over the local kids. Acceptable morality kept the Breen Office happy; audiences too were happy, because the Cagney of *G-Men* had given way to the old, devil-may-care Cagney of *The Public Enemy*.

These were the best of the crime movies of the thirties, but there were many others, including detective series, with such sleuths as Hildegarde Withers (engaging comedy with ZaSu Pitts or Helen

Broderick); Mr Moto (where poor plots and indifferent support tended to waste Peter Lorre); Perry Mason (better plots, and the forceful Warren William in the lead); and above all Charlie Chan.

From 1931 until 1938, when he died, the Swedish actor Warner Oland was the perfect incarnation of the aphoristic and ever-perceptive Chinese detective, with Keye Luke, who really was Chinese, as the brash and pushy "Number One Son". At least two of the Chans were really first-rate movies: in *Charlie Chan at the Opera* (1936) Karloff as an opera singer escaped from an asylum gives Oland a real rival to play against, while *Charlie Chan on Broadway* (1937), the best of all, has a diabolically clever plot raced through, in true thirties style, at breakneck speed and with perfect clarity.

Petty crime?

Finally, a few not-quite-greats, but films which, long unseen, stay in the mind as particular joys. *Death on the Diamond* (1934) is a baseball mystery directed, strangely, by comedy specialist Edward Sedgwick. There is a marvelously macabre 1937 MGM piece called *Under Cover of Night*, which has that master of sardonic lordliness, Henry Daniell, cast as a crazed professor who knocks off half the faculty before they catch up with him; this was directed by George B. Seitz, a great master of the small movie, also responsible for such good little MGM thrillers as *Absolute Quiet* (1936), *The Thirteenth Chair* (1937) and *Kind Lady* (1935). Sadly, the studio never let Seitz loose on their prestige productions, some of which really needed livening up. Other joys include *Night Must Fall* (1937), with the excellent Rosalind Russell, but suave Robert Montgomery hardly convincing as a homicidal Welsh pageboy, and *The Doorway to Hell* (1930), with gentle, idealistic Lew Ayres just as oddly cast as a hoodlum, but getting away with it.

The Berkeley Touch

Chapter 3

As soon as sound came in the studios leapt at the opportunity to create something entirely new — the musical. The first offerings were very simple. Studios used most of their stars — often regardless of their singing or dancing skills — and sometimes a whole bevy of directors to mount a lavish revue. A storyline was replaced by a series of star turns. Such were Warners' *The Show of Shows* (1929), MGM's *The Hollywood Revue of 1929*, and *Paramount on Parade* (1930). But in 1929 there were two entirely successful attempts at better things. *The Broadway Melody*, directed by Harry Beaumont, contain good numbers, a strong story, and a heart-rending performance from Bessie Love, while Ernst Lubitsch's *The Love Parade* had the pairing of Maurice Chevalier and Jeanette MacDonald, and enough sparkle to suggest that Lubitsch would soon make musicals as engaging as his silent comedies.

The delights of Lubitsch

With *Monte Carlo* (1930) the promise was fulfilled. MacDonald sang "Beyond the Blue Horizon" aboard a speeding train — the wheels whirred, the rails danced, and happy workers in the passing fields joined in the chorus; the cinematic musical was born. In her Paramount days MacDonald was an enchanting comedienne with a wicked twinkle in her eye; she needed a director like Lubitsch or Mamoulian to keep the twinkle there, and when she later went on to MGM, who saw her as a ladylike partner for stolid Nelson Eddy, a thirties treasure was lost.

In 1931 came *The Smiling Lieutenant:* Lubitsch again, the elegant swagger of the Paramount look, and one delicious number that had bubbling Claudette Colbert urging the staid princess of Miriam Hopkins to "Jazz up Your Lingerie". Lubitsch's next musical, *One Hour with You* (1932), an unnecessary remake of his finest silent comedy, *The Marriage Circle* (1924), was curiously lifeless; perhaps it suffered from the stresses that had led to the removal of the original director, George Cukor, after two weeks' shooting, but for whatever reason, the movie tried too hard and too consciously for gaiety, and fell with a thud.

However, Lubitsch's fifth musical, but this time at MGM, *The Merry Widow* (1934), was a triumph all the way, though it didn't find immediate popularity with audiences — by now conditioned to the totally different Warners musical style — and was compared unfavorably by critics with Stroheim's silent version. Lubitsch had Chevalier and MacDonald again, joined by two superlative comedians in Edward Everett Horton and Una Merkel, and the marvelous Léhar score coming from the screen (not, as it had for Stroheim, from the

Right: *Tap-dancing queen Eleanor Powell serenaded by the American navy in Roy Del Ruth's lavish 1936 musical* **Born to Dance,** *made at MGM. Miss Powell was supported in this innocent froth by James Stewart, Virginia Bruce and Una Merkel.*

orchestra pit). Wisely, he didn't aim for the underlying gravity of the Stroheim film, but was content to mix Ruritanian court with Parisian restaurant, ironic comedy with lyrical romance, and make the whole an irresistibly heady delight.

On 42nd Street...

In the early months of 1933 there was turmoil at the Burbank studios of Warner Brothers. The Depression had hit the studio so hard that it inflicted a 50 per cent salary cut on all employees. In March 1933, amid the rancor, disaffection and talk of court action this caused, the studio released a movie of boundless energy and devastating wit, a movie that looks and sounds as though made by a studio without a care in the world – the immortal *42nd Street*. The film loosed on the world the intricate exuberance of Busby Berkeley's choreography – something entirely new and daring and, at its best, a perfect blending of cinema and dance.

Nowadays people talk, and write, as though *42nd Street* were a Berkeley film alone, but that is to miss much of its glory. There were Berkeley numbers, some of them even better than *42nd Street*'s, in a dozen other films of the period, yet none of those films is as inexhaustibly rewarding as this one. *42nd Street* is a Berkeley triumph in which he directed the numbers; the remaining three-quarters of the film was the work of Lloyd Bacon who directed a strong story and dialogue with tang and bite and a cast of superb straight actors (with the exception of Ruby Keeler, who made up for it with her charm). That was the essence of the trick, and while Warners brought it off to some degree in other movies, it never worked as well as here.

Far left: *Jeanette MacDonald and Maurice Chevalier in* **The Merry Widow** *(1934). For this film director Ernst Lubitsch left Paramount for MGM, but he took his stars with him, with all their sparkle and lightness. In the film Maurice Chevalier* **(right)** *plays the part of Danilo. Here, the ladies of Maxim's establishment decide that he deserves their closest attentions.*

Above: *The Goldwyn Girls performing a Busby Berkeley number on their way to the bath in* **The Kid From Spain** *(1932). Compare the insufferable coyness of this line-up with the exuberance of the "Waterfall" number on pages 2–3. The Kid was Eddie Cantor, whose strident vaudeville style didn't always work on film.*

Consider that cast: Warner Baxter as the hard driving producer; Bebe Daniels, a great silent star, as the elegant if aging lead; Ginger Rogers and Una Merkel as two chorines on the make, one a transparently fake grande dame, the other pure Brooklyn, with an acid tongue; chirpy little George E. Stone as the dance director, earthy Allen Jenkins stage managing, and a host more. *42nd Street* could even afford to toss in a talented player of hoodlums like Jack LaRue for a half-minute appearance, while in the original cut there was a cameo of an old actor played by none other than Henry B. Walthall, the Little Colonel of *The Birth of a Nation* (1915). Unhappily, Walthall's part vanished from the release prints, save for one unexplained glimpse of him by the stage door.

Busy hands and Busby Berkeley

The pre-code dialogue is still a great delight, some of it so fast and casual that you pick up fresh lines at almost every viewing. "You've got the busiest hands," exclaims Merkel as she is swung back and forwards by a chorus boy. And in the same scene there is this – rather risqué – exchange: "Where you sitting, dearie, where you sitting?" asks the boy. "On a flagpole – on a flagpole", she replies as she sits on his lap. "Afraid I've gotta run", says a chorine as she lifts her skirt for the producer, and "First door on the left," cracks her neighbor. Cynicism pervades. "Okay those three on the left, Mr Marsh," says Stone, meaning Rogers, Merkel and Keeler. "If I were you I'd keep 'em." "I suppose if I don't, you'll have to," Baxter fires back, keeping them.

Busby Berkeley had been a Broadway dance director before Samuel Goldwyn called him to Hollywood to choreograph *Whoopee*

Far left: *Lyda Roberti and Eddie Cantor in* **The Kid From Spain** *(1932). Roberti, a vivacious blonde from Poland, enlivened a number of Hollywood musicals before suffering a fatal heart attack in 1938.* **The Kid From Spain,** *zestfully directed by comedy expert Leo McCarey, was easily Cantor's best sound film.*

Main picture: *Producer Warner Baxter lectures novice chorine Ruby Keeler in* **42nd Street** *(1933). In spite of this unpromising start, Keeler keeps her job, and ends up making the classic transition from chorus-girl to star.*

Above: *George Stone and the chorus line in the same film. Another carefully posed still for cinema use, with Keeler, just another girl at this stage of the film, conveniently at the head of the line.*

(1930) and other musicals for Eddie Cantor. He contributed attractive, routine chorus-line scenes for these films. With his move to Warners Berkeley was transformed. He moved his camera with a fine abandon along and over and under his innumerable girls; he shot them from above as the complex patterns of his kaleidoscope revolved; he played tricks with waterfalls and sleeping-cars, moving pianos, and violins glowing in the dark.

Berkeley also told stories in the best of his numbers, stories that played on every kind of emotion, sometimes most unexpected ones. In *Footlight Parade* (1933) Cagney prowls through sleazy Chinese dives "looking for his Shanghai Lil"; Wini Shaw falls to her death from a high window in *Gold Diggers of 1935* (1935), playing a doomed night club girl who sings her "Lullaby of Broadway"; and there is a sharp, savage killing in the climactic ballet of *42nd Street*. In another mood, in Mervyn LeRoy's *Gold Diggers of 1933* (1933), Berkeley's camera glides past the beaten faces of a Depression breadline, while the figure of Joan Blondell and the voice of Etta Moten evoke pity for "My Forgotten Man".

Berkeley's comic sense could be alarming at times. One of his trademarks was the introduction into a musical number of a lecherous toddler, gleefully played by Billy Barty, who licked his lips at the goings-on he should never have been allowed to see. Barty's best moment came in the "Pettin' in the Park" number from *Gold Diggers of 1933*. Berkeley encased his chorines in tight-fitting metal sheaths for this one. Dick Powell finds that this frustrates his designs on Keeler, whereupon Barty sidles up and presents him with a can-opener.

Berkeley duly became a full director. He was in charge of the whole of *Gold Diggers of 1935*, and later moved to MGM and Twentieth Century-Fox, but his work there seldom had the sheer cinematic flair of the early thirties days.

Left: *Chorus-girls and boys in the "Pettin' in the Park" number from* **Gold Diggers of 1933.** *A musical born of the Depression,* **Gold Diggers** *was directed by Mervyn LeRoy, Warners' specialist in movies with a social comment.*

Below: *The Goldwyn Girls who starred in* **Whoopee!** *(1930),* **Palmy Days** *(1932) and* **Roman Scandals** *(1933), as well as* **The Kid From Spain** *(1932).*

The musical takes wings

MGM turned seriously to musicals in the mid-thirties with *Broadway Melody of 1936* (1935), *Born to Dance* (1936) and *Rosalie* (1937). The great strength of these was the astonishing tap-dancing of Eleanor Powell. There are some memorable songs ("Broadway Rhythm" from the first, "I've Got You Under My Skin" from the second), ingenious sets and no expense spared. Far from masterpieces, these films are extremely happy diversions, as are the teenage musicals with Mickey Rooney and Judy Garland which appeared at the end of the decade.

The studio's most famous musical is *The Great Ziegfeld* (1936); the musical interludes were grandiose but not particularly memorable, and the movie didn't actually need them. It had other things to offer: William Powell as the great man himself, Luise Rainer and Myrna Loy as Anna Held and Billie Burke, and one of the rare film appearances of the Broadway comedienne Fanny Brice, the "Funny Girl" herself.

RKO contributed richly to the thirties musical with their Fred Astaire and Ginger Rogers series. In all, the pair danced in 10 films beginning with supporting roles in *Flying Down to Rio* (1933). The movie is best remembered for the final aerial ballet, with dance director Dave Gould's chorus gyrating on the wings of airplanes in flight. Earlier in this film Fred and Ginger danced the "Carioca", and a chapter in film history began.

Fred Astaire had been a Broadway star since 1917, but had made just one film, *Dancing Lady* (1933). Rogers had been in movies rather longer, with her sharp comedy in *42nd Street* the culmination of four years playing leads in small pictures and supporting roles in larger ones. She found Astaire, the chemistry between them worked, and a new kind of musical was born.

Astaire and Rogers didn't really rely too much on the eye-catching gimmickry of their occasional all-over-the-furniture routines. Other dancers could do those just as well. Their finest numbers were those in which a romantic elegance had full play, and fluid movement and a depth of affection extraordinary in a musical made the screen throb with delight. This happened in numbers like Cole Porter's "Night and Day" from *The Gay Divorcee* (1934), Jerome Kern's "Lovely to Look At" from *Roberta* (1935) and his "The Way You Look Tonight" from *Swing Time* (1936). Perhaps the most entrancing of them all is Irving Berlin's "Let's Face the Music and Dance" from *Follow the Fleet* (1936). Fred and Ginger were lucky in their composers (the four movies cited had the three best), in their directors (especially the gifted Mark Sandrich), in their art director (RKO's Van Nest Polglase, a great hand at the shining black and white surfaces that set the pair off to perfection), and in their regular supporting casts (proud, pained Eric Blore; waspish continental Erik Rhodes; and down-to-earth Helen Broderick). Their films are star movies if ever any were. Not only in their dancing did they suit one another perfectly — their personalities matched as well, with Ginger's gritty common sense anchoring Fred's more wayward flights. It was noticeable, too, that when Fred's tendency to cocksureness got the better of him, as with his gum-chewing sailor in *Follow the Fleet*, the warmth that was expected from him was absent.

Main picture: *The extraordinary "Remember My Forgotten Man" number from **Gold Diggers of 1933**. The musical shocked many because it spelled out that war brought poverty and degradation — some reviewers even suggested that the song should be eliminated. Joan Blondell, seen here, mimed — Etta Moten provided the voice.*

Top right: *Busby Berkeley's kaleidoscope at work in the title number of **Dames** (1934), directed by Ray Enright. The last of Berkeley's great quartet, **Dames** had an extremely funny script, with Hugh Herbert and ZaSu Pitts as Purity Leaguers gunning for Broadway.*

Showboat sails again

In 1936 Universal made one of the period's finest musicals, the second of the cinema's three versions of *Showboat*. The 1929 version, coming at the transition between silence and sound, had done its best, preceding an essentially silent film with a sound prologue featuring singers from the stage production. These included Helen Morgan who, in the 1936 film, played the tragic half-caste Julie, the last film but one of a career that in real life was as sad as that of the unhappy, fallen women she played so movingly.

The 1936 version was directed by James Whale, unused to musicals but the only top-notch director at Universal and an inspired choice. Whale had Irene Dunne for his lead, a sweet singer and a considerable actress, both in romantic drama and in the screwball comedy that was to be so popular in the late thirties; he had Paul Robeson singing "Ol' Man River", where the camerawork was as striking as the song; genial old Charles Winninger as the show boat's skipper; and that formidable lady Helen Westley as his wife. Dunne, Robeson and Morgan, with Allan Jones as the handsome scapegrace who comes back to Dunne after the years, do full justice to Jerome Kern's superlative score, the emotion is nicely managed without becoming over-powering, and the film shows that stage musical comedy, given a director with Whale's eye for composition, works as well, if not better, on the screen.

Universal's Deanna Durbin musicals, starting with *Three Smart Girls* (1937), rescued the studio from financial crisis. She was 14 when the first film was made, and instantly became immensely popular. She sang with patent enjoyment, acted with no trace of child-star affectation or winsomeness, and could make the crustiest spectator give in. In Deanna's day, the great W.C. Fields was also a denizen of Universal; the studio never teamed them, and wisely so, for Deanna would have broken down even that great child-hater's defences, and done irreparable harm to his image. For the rest of the thirties Universal found her fresh and lively vehicles, with *Mad about Music* (1938) just about the best of them. Later they did become a great deal thinner, and it took a brave venture into *film noir* with Robert Siodmak's *Christmas Holiday* (1945) to give Deanna a success to rank with those early ones.

Twentieth Century-Fox's prestige musical of the decade was Henry King's *Alexander's Ragtime Band* that was released in 1938. Since then the film has been so beset by copyright problems that it has never been revived. It was a stylish, tastefully mounted production, too slight emotionally to engage the director fully (in King's best films feeling ran deep) but giving Alice Faye and her husky contralto far more scope than Fox's routine musicals had ever done. But Alice's gently winning ways – no one ever wrinkled a nose as fetchingly as Faye – make most Fox musicals enjoyable, and her eventual replacement as the studio's top musical star by the brassy Betty Grable was a symptom of the rougher days that lay ahead.

Good and bad notes

This chapter ends where it began, with Paramount. For Paramount's musical history contained rather more than the work of Ernst Lubitsch. For instance, the studio made a lot of really dreadful comedies with music starring Bing Crosby, who, though a fine singer and a cosy personality, simply couldn't carry the terrible stories and lifeless direction he was lumbered with. As examples of how dire a thirties musical could be, look at two characteristic Paramount efforts, *We're Not Dressing* (1934) and *Doctor Rhythm* (1938). The first of these creaking horrors had a superb comedienne in Carole Lombard, the second the uniquely witty Beatrice Lillie, but all to no avail. Paramount thought Crosby's numbers would do, but they didn't. However, the studio made money without really trying. When they did try, as with the Lubitsch films, the results could be spectacular, and they include two musicals from Rouben Mamoulian that far outweigh all the misbegotten ventures.

Left and right: *Ilona Massey in MGM's* **Rosalie** *(1937). The studio's musical style was not really formed until the forties, but the thirties did provide occasional pleasures.* **Rosalie** *was the first of Hungarian Ilona Massey's few American films.*
Top: *More Berkeley ingenuity. In* **Dames** *(1934) cut-outs of Ruby Keeler's face formed themselves into fantastic patterns at a twitch of the maestro's wand.*

Mamoulian made his first five films for Paramount between 1929 and 1933. His debut film, *Applause*, though not primarily a musical, had Helen Morgan songs; the fourth, *Love Me Tonight* (1933), could well be the finest of all thirties musicals. It looks like a Lubitsch film, with the same stars, Chevalier and MacDonald, the same sophisticated art direction from Hans Dreier, the same Ruritanian setting, although this time it is nominally Paris and the country around. But Mamoulian outdid the master with this perfect jewel of a film. The whole movie is a piece of music, from the opening in the city with its soundtrack filled with the noises of Paris coming to life, recalling, but effortlessly surpassing, René Clair's *Sous les Toits de Paris/Under the Roofs of Paris* (1930), into the first song, the intoxicating "Isn't It Romantic?" sung by Chevalier as a hard-up tailor, and carried on enthusiastically by taxi-drivers, musicians, soldiers and gypsies, through an hour and a half of enchantment.

The film contains such startling pleasures as dignified old C. Aubrey Smith actually joining in a song ("The son of a gun's a tailor"),

moving on to a climax that parodies early movies yet creates its own delirious charm as MacDonald races to stand defiantly across a railroad track to stop the train that is carrying Chevalier away. That stance encapsulates all the undaunted wit and pride that Lubitsch and Mamoulian, and no one else, managed to uncover in this delectable actress.

Below: *Paul Robeson sings "Ol' Man River" in one of the most famous scenes from James Whale's* **Showboat** *(1936). The Second of three versions, this featured a superb score by Jerome Kern.*

Left: *Ginger Rogers and Fred Astaire in* **Shall We Dance?** *(1937), directed by Mark Sandrich, and with a score by George and Ira Gershwin. Note the look which Astaire casts towards Rogers. A posed shot it may well be, but that look sums up the sympathy that was there between the two.*

There was more, too, in *Love Me Tonight:* Charles Butterworth, ineffable silly-ass of thirties comedies, tumbling off a ladder as he woos MacDonald and "falling flat on his flute"; the trio of elderly aunts who provide a pessimistic commentary on the action; even the odd shift into verse dialogue when the movie gets so airborne that prose won't do. And there is Myrna Loy, still the unregenerate Myrna of the days before she "married" Powell, but a thoroughly nice girl too, strictly brought up by her uncle Aubrey Smith. Thoroughly nice, but just a little overfond of men. She is sitting alone when Charles Ruggles bursts in. "Can you go for a doctor?" says a worried Ruggles. "Certainly," Loy whips back. "Send him right in!"

Mamoulian came back to Paramount in 1937 for one more musical, *High, Wide and Handsome,* an offbeat movie with marvelous moments. It had a Jerome Kern score, Irene Dunne in spirited form to sing it, and a story that only Mamoulian could have lifted up so easily into the artifices of the musical without sacrificing a lot of its dramatic force. It is a very good story – a sort of Western, though set in Pennsylvania, about oil-prospectors and the wicked railroad tycoons who are threatening their land. It had good Western type he-men too – Randolph Scott, Charles Bickford, Alan Hale – and it would have made a nice John Ford movie. Instead it had Mamoulian – and as a result it took off.

*Below left: Ethel Merman in **Alexander's Ragtime Band** (1938). One of the greatest musical stars of the American theater, Merman made relatively few films, mostly ephemeral. In another scene from the same film, **below,** Alice Faye and Tyrone Power are on the verge of wonderful things.*

Fantasy Thirties Style

Chapter 4

What the thirties called horror films are not really that at all. They do all kinds of things, but they do not horrify. The thirties films send an occasional pleasurable shiver down the spine; they can amaze, but not alarm, divert, but not discomfort. If there are exceptions to this, they are films like Tod Browning's *Freaks* (1932), which set out from the beginning to do something more than shock. Thirties horror is more properly fantasy, and as fantasy it roams far and wide, from islands inhabited by prehistoric creatures, islands where men hunted men or turned beasts into men, to hilltop castles in Eastern Europe, gloomy laboratories in Paris or New York, and decaying, rainswept old mansions in remote parts of Wales.

Return of the vampire

Universal set the pace and kept up the fashion longest. In 1931 they released Tod Browning's version of *Dracula*. Bram Stoker's classic novel had been filmed before, by F.W. Murnau in Germany, as *Nosferatu* (1922). Murnau's feeling for space, and the silent cinema's unique ability to lull its audiences into dream, made *Nosferatu* into a masterpiece; Browning's film was less ambitious, but powerful enough on its own terms. Garrett Fort's screenplay was derived from a stage version rather than the original novel, which meant that the latter half in particular, after the traveling to and from the castle in Transylvania, was overburdened with talk about which Browning could do little. But the casting of the title role made the film. Lon Chaney had been the first choice, and inevitably so, for Browning had directed many of Chaney's silent films with enormous success. But Chaney died before production started, and the part passed to the Hungarian actor Bela Lugosi, who had previously played Dracula on Broadway back in 1927.

For the rest of his life, Lugosi's career was haunted by memories of this one part. He fitted it to perfection. The lilting, slightly accented voice, the piercing eyes, the proud stance, the measured walk, all made Lugosi's Count so devilishly effective that the unsatisfactory script ceased to matter. Lugosi's voice made lines like the opening "I am – Dracula" and the invocation of the wolves in "Listen to them – children of the night – what music they make!" burn in the mind. Visually, too, there were splendid moments, like the awakening of Dracula's brides, gliding gauzily about their dark tomb, and the crossing to England in a ship of the dead. And Lugosi did not lack support. Helen Chandler was the fragile and lovely heroine who disappeared from the screen all too soon – her wistful beauty would have made her a great star in silent days; Edward Van Sloan was the vampire hunter Van Helsing and, as the crazed, insect-eating Renfield, there was Dwight Frye. The last two players reveled in eccentric characterizations, the stranger the better.

*King Kong fights off a huge prehistoric bird which is attacking Fay Wray in Merian C. Cooper's famous production of **King Kong** (1933).*

Made for Karloff

Frye was around again, this time as the Baron's dwarfish assistant, in *Frankenstein*, which at the end of the year was Universal's second, and even greater, success. Again there were one or two last-minute changes of plan. Lugosi turned down the role of the Monster, fearing, it is said, that his face would be unrecognizable behind make-up, with the result that Boris Karloff, hitherto a character heavy, became a star; and for reasons unclear the direction was taken from the Frenchman Robert Florey (who was offered *The Murders in the Rue Morgue* as a consolation prize in 1932) and given to James Whale, then a newcomer with only *Journey's End* and one other film behind him. *Frankenstein* would lift Whale above Browning as the thirties master of fantasy.

As before, the lead actor dominated the film. Unhampered by the make-up – an elaborate job by Universal's master of the craft, Jack Pierce, which took hours each day to apply – Karloff managed to make the Monster an uncanny mingling of the tender and the grotesque, never playing overtly for sympathy yet obtaining a great deal. Everyone remembers the scene by the lakeside with the little girl, shot by Whale with a moving reticence; no less striking was a scene in total contrast, when the Monster was brought to life. Universal's art director, Charles D. Hall, excelled himself in the magnificent scene with the platform bearing the Monster rising up into the stormy sky from the cavernous workshop with all its outlandish equipment. Whale and Karloff made the creature's subsequent first bemused moments into something touching and wonderful.

Left: *Boris Karloff as the Monster in James Whale's* **Frankenstein** *(1931). When the film came out, Bioscope's reviewer found it "a rather crudely constructed blood curdler", deplored the artificial sets, and even spotted creases in the backcloth at one point. But the years have made it an undisputed classic, creases and all.*

Right: *Bela Lugosi threatens the sleeping Frances Dade in Tod Browning's* **Dracula** *(1931). Lugosi had appeared in films in his native Hungary, in Germany and (since 1923) in America. This one film transformed him from a character player into a star.*

53

Making the most of their good fortune, Universal turned out three more "horror" films in 1932. In *The Mummy* Karloff is swathed in bandages but of a different kind, and plays a deadly ancient Egyptian at large in modern Cairo. A little tamer than its predecessors, it has a notable moment when the Mummy first stirs from its long sleep, and the later plot developments, with Karloff now incarnated as an elderly priest, give the actor a chance to change key to the silkily sinister.

Murders in the Rue Morgue has little in common with the Edgar Allan Poe story it claims to tell (none of the variants played on *The Black Cat* had much to do with him either), but the stylized sets could have graced a German silent, and Robert Florey, an accomplished director whose talents the studios shamefully misused, handled the whole thing with an engaging lightness of touch. Lugosi plays Doctor Mirakle, one of the first of the "mad doctors" so numerous in the thirties fantasy cycle, who was seeking a human bride for the gorilla he exhibited as a fairground attraction. He unfortunately insisted on injecting the poor girls with ape blood to see if they were suitable – a precaution that seldom turned out well. Nonsense it was, but it was good fun nonetheless.

Left: *Gloria Stuart in James Whale's* **The Old Dark House** *(1932). The arm belongs to Boris Karloff as the dumb butler, Morgan. Stuart and a young Mervyn Douglas were a couple marooned in the strange house, and Charles Laughton played a self-made business man.*

Above: *Bela Lugosi as Dr Mirakle, having trouble with his ape in* **Murders in the Rue Morgue** *(1932). Universal retained little of Edgar Allan Poe's story beyond having the heroine's mother's body pushed up a chimney!*

Ghouls and ghosts

James Whale followed *Frankenstein* with *The Old Dark House* (1932), transforming J. B. Priestley's novel *Benighted* into something its creator would hardly have recognized. Derived more essentially from such twenties movies as *The Cat and the Canary* (1927), the film transports half a dozen characters marooned by floods to a curious house in the Welsh mountains inhabited by a dumb and malevolent butler (Karloff), a centenarian baronet (played by an elderly woman, Elspeth Dudgeon, although John Dudgeon is the name on the credits) and a mad arsonist; Ernest Thesiger as the master of the house presides, and Thesiger's usual line, that of a sweetly demented academic, makes him seem a model of normality in comparison.

The visitors include a young Melvyn Douglas, and a Charles Laughton still making his way as a screen actor and in rich form here as a self-made Lancashire businessman. Legal difficulties kept the film off the screen for many years. On its recent reappearance it looked better than ever – shot through with ironic comedy and an ingenuous delight in the grotesque.

Other studios were quick to follow Universal's lead: 1932 was also the year of Paramount's version of *Dr Jekyll and Mr Hyde*, of MGM's *Freaks* and *The Mask of Fu Manchu*, and of RKO's *The Most Dangerous Game*, all of them fantasies in their widely differing ways. This *Dr Jekyll and Mr Hyde*, directed by Rouben Mamoulian, is much the best of the surviving versions of the story and, unless some miracle brings back Murnau's 1920 film, is likely to remain so. As always with Mamoulian, the film looks magnificent – a totally convincing panorama of Victorian London, marvelously shot by the great cameraman Karl Struss. It has Fredric March in the dual role, displaying as Hyde a ferocity that owes far more to the actor than to the make-up (and is worlds away from the serenity that was the actor's normal stock in trade); it includes a splendid slut played by Miriam Hopkins as the girl Hyde kills; and it displays Mamoulian's novel approach, beginning with a subjective camera sequence, with the audience as Jekyll's eyes, that had many imitators.

The Mask of Fu Manchu is a rather stiffly directed film (credited to

Below left: *Fredric March and Miriam Hopkins in Rouben Mamoulian's version of* **Dr Jekyll and Mr Hyde** *(1932). A staple of popular cinema ever since the Selig Polyscope company made the first version back in 1908, the story provided great roles for Conrad Veidt, John Barrymore, Fredric March and Spencer Tracy. March's performance won him a share in the Best Actor Award that year, with Wallace Beery equally honored for* **The Champ.**

Right: *March drains the potion to convince the sceptical Lanyon (Holmes Herbert), out of shot, that Jekyll and Hyde are the same. (When Hollywood wanted sturdy common sense, Herbert, an English actor who had been a romantic lead in the silents, was usually there to answer the call.)*

Inset below: *A tense moment for Boris Karloff and Gloria Stuart in* **The Old Dark House** *released in 1932.*

Charles Brabin, but in fact partly the work of Charles Vidor), but has a performance of gloating relish from Karloff as the megalomaniac Chinaman, and one to match it from Myrna Loy as Fu Manchu's daughter, enthusiastically devoted to love and torture alike. This is a film of joyful wickedness, owing almost everything to the actors, and lucky to slip through in those final years of lax censorship.

Beauties, beasts and freaks

Freaks is the most bizarre of all Tod Browning's creations – and his masterpiece. It is the story of a group of fairground freaks, played in the main by real freaks, who wear their deformity with a touching pride. The film tells the story of a heartless jest played upon a midget (Harry Earles) by a callous trapeze artiste (former silent star Olga Baclanova) and her strong-man lover. In a terrible climax the whole company of freaks creeps and slithers across the dark fairground to take a macabre vengeance; Baclanova is by some unholy alchemy translated to a freak herself – half-woman, half-chicken.

Beside this, *The Most Dangerous Game* is a piece of healthy outdoor exercise, with a crazed hunter (Leslie Banks) pursuing his human quarry (Joel McCrea) through the *King Kong* jungle. The two films were made back-to-back on the RKO lot, with Ernest B. Schoedsack, co-director of *Kong*, in charge of the lesser movie too, and Robert Armstrong bravely acting away in both with co-star Fay Wray, never one to be daunted by man or beast.

The glory of Schoedsack and Merian C. Cooper's *King Kong* (1933) remains undimmed by the years. The screen's most familiar story needs no retelling. The film is the kind of triumph that only the studio system, with its technical resources and its array of attendant experts, could produce – the stop-motion animation of the old master Willis O'Brien, ingenious process photography, Murray Spivack's astonishing sound effects and Max Steiner's lively score. In addition, *Kong* is a marvelously structured film. There is a quiet

Top: *Claude Rains in James Whale's* **The Invisible Man** *(1933). A stage actor in his mid-forties at the time of this, his film debut, Rains was perhaps the best actor never to win an Academy Award.*
Main picture: *The spikes are nasty enough, but the walls that hold them slide inwards as well. Jean Hersholt is the victim in* **The Mask of Fu Manchu** *(1932).*
Inset right: *Myrna Loy, who started out portraying Oriental villainesses, Charles Starrett and Boris Karloff in a scene from the same film.*

beginning in the city and on the ship, drawn out almost, but not quite, to the point of impatience; then the arrival at the lost island and Kong's appearance, before the pace really quickens with a return to New York. There are just a few moments to gather one's shaken nerves, before being plunged into the effrontery of the final scenes on the Elevated Railroad and the Empire State Building. *King Kong* is thirties film-making at its swaggering best – self-assured and self-sufficient, inviting admiration and commanding belief.

Universal's *The Invisible Man*, directed by James Whale in 1933, would have led the field in most other years. Once again a leading role changed hands at the last minute. Rightly, Boris Karloff thought his voice unsuited to a part that would stand or fall by that, and gave way to Claude Rains, an English stage actor making his first film. Rains' voice has just the right suggestion of edgy nerves and barely controlled threat. John P. Fulton's special effects are smoothly executed without distracting the viewer from the human tragedy; and if the English villagers and their picture-book village are not particularly convincing, it is after all not a movie where reality matters very much. Claude Rains became one of the great character actors.

Tod Browning retired at the end of the thirties, but two of his last films kept his reputation high to the last. *The Mark of the Vampire* (1935) plays a gentle joke on *Dracula*, with Lugosi back in the vampire's cloak, and accompanied by a dark beauty (Carol Borland)

clearly as nefarious as her friend. Browning gives their sequences a gliding, almost balletic poetry that turns out to be entirely suitable, for the pair are eventually revealed as actors, hired to put the fear of God into some poor wretch.

Browning followed up with something better still – *The Devil Doll* (1936). Lionel Barrymore emerges from a long, unjust imprisonment, stumbles upon deranged Henry B. Walthall, the inventor of tiny dolls that carry out orders, and uses the dolls to destroy the men who framed him. Disguised in what looks very like Lon Chaney's old lady outfit from *The Unholy Three* (1925), Barrymore steers the dolls on their deadly missions with ill-concealed glee, while out-sized furniture is ingeniously used to create the necessary illusion.

Above: *Rafaela Ottiano and Lionel Barrymore in Tod Browning's* **The Devil Doll** *(1936). These toys are innocent enough: the lethal ones were actors skilfully photographed against huge props and furniture, the technique used later in* **The Incredible Shrinking Man** *(1957). Browning managed the trick beautifully, and the dolls carried a genuine threat.*

Right: *Bela Lugosi in another Browning classic,* **The Mark of the Vampire** *(1935).*

Bride for a monster

Whale's *The Bride of Frankenstein* (1935) achieves the near impossible – a sequel that is even better than a good original. Karloff's monster gains in pathos as he learns more of the hostile world that surrounds him, and he has an immensely moving scene with O.P. Heggie as a blind hermit who welcomes and entertains him. Elsa Lanchester is Karloff's bride (not Frankenstein's, in spite of the title), and Ernest Thesiger as a sacked university professor (and another creator of living dolls, this time kept safely in glass jars) shows that the gentlemanly way to treat Karloff is the right one, offering him a cigar ("my only weakness") with true old-world courtesy.

There were simply so many films released in the thirties that some of the best slipped by unnoticed, shown as the bottom half of a double bill. One such movie was Edgar G. Ulmer's *The Black Cat* (1934). Much later, Ulmer, a one-time assistant of Murnau who made films in half a dozen countries and languages, including some engaging thirties movies shot in New York in Yiddish, acquired such a considerable reputation as a cult director that *The Black Cat* and other of his early films were properly looked at for the first time.

The Black Cat proved a discovery indeed, and one of the most startlingly original of all thirties films. Set in a castle in Austria, standing over the carnage of a world war battlefield – an inspired invention that lent a feeling of surrounding death to the whole movie – the film brought Karloff and Lugosi together, with Lugosi in a rare sympathe-

tic role as a scientist seeking out the man who has stolen his wife and ruined him. Karloff has, in fact, done rather worse than that, and the two play out a deadly contest (with time out for a little Satanism and necrophilia) that has an apocalyptic end, with the flaying of Karloff and the eruption of all the explosives that still mine the foundations of the house. Perhaps this one alone was, genuinely, a horror film. Certainly Ulmer and his cinematographer, John Mescall, who had also shot *The Invisible Man*, gave it a sustained atmosphere of menace that makes it disturbing watching even today.

MGM's *Mad Love*, directed by Karl Freund in 1935, introduced Peter Lorre to the American cinema, and gave him the role of a surgeon who grafts the hands of an executed murderer to the arms of a pianist injured in a train wreck, with results not entirely therapeutic. It was all rather second-hand, being the remake of a 1925 Austrian film that had combined the talents of Robert Wiene, director of *Das Kabinett des Dr Caligari/The Cabinet of Dr Caligari* (1919), and of two great actors, Werner Krauss as the surgeon and Conrad Veidt as the pianist, but few of its thirties audiences had seen the original – *Orlacs Hände/The Hands of Orlac* (1924) – and Freund's version had many merits. He had worked as photographer on many German films of the great years, and here as director made such striking use of distorted shadows and extravagant architecture that his return to photography (he never directed again) seems a curious decision.

Peter Lorre **(above)** makes his Hollywood debut as
an extremely sinister surgeon in Karl Freund's
Mad Love (1935), while **(left)** Frances Drake is
put to the torture. Freund's photographic credits
included **The Last Laugh** and **Variety** in Germany,
Dracula and **The Good Earth** in America.
Between 1932 and 1935 he directed eight
films, but only this one and **The Mummy**
fully exploited his visual sense.

Right: Colin Clive, Elsa Lanchester, and
Boris Karloff in **The Bride of
Frankenstein** (1935).

Few films of the kind were made in the later thirties. By around 1936 the impetus of *Dracula* and the rest seemed exhausted, but still the occasional pleasure came to light. Warners were never considered as one of the main fantasy film studios, but they had had their moments with films like *Doctor X* (1932) and *The Mystery of the Wax Museum* (1933), both directed by Michael Curtiz. The latter was shot in the early two-strip Technicolor that was so successful in creating a threatening ambience.

Now, at the end of the cycle, Curtiz made one of the most impressive of Karloff's films, *The Walking Dead* (1936). As yet another innocent man seeking revenge, Karloff differed from others of the kind in that he actually had been electrocuted and restored to life by the wizardry of scientist Edmund Gwenn. One by one the guilty men die, always with Karloff around, using some sixth sense to ease them gently to their doom. In spite of the many deaths it encompasses, *The Walking Dead* is a quiet and understated film, and none the worse for that.

Outward bound course

Films of pure fantasy, without a touch of horror, are rare in the thirties. *Outward Bound* (1930) is a version of a stage play by Sutton Vane, set on a ship taking the recently dead to an appointment with the Examiner who will decide their destination. There is far too much dialogue just two short years into sound (stage plays were dangerous material in this respect) and a shamefully contrived happy end, but two pieces of good casting help to suspend disbelief. Leslie Howard in his first sound film (his last silent had been in 1920) plays a scapegoat son, now happily reunited with his adoring old mother, with the muted charm that would become famous, while Helen Chandler is a suicide as poignant as could be without a trace of morbid self-pity.

Finally, Paramount and Mitchell Leisen's *Death Takes a Holiday* (1934) provides a lesson in how a stage play should be transferred to the screen. The play, an adaptation from the Spanish by Maxwell Anderson of *Winterset* (1936), was further adapted by Anderson. It has a marvelous subject. Death comes to earth to find out why men fear him so greatly, and what there is in this world that they so much prefer. While Death is thus on holiday, no one can die, whatever illness or accident befalls him. A lesser film would have made a great deal of that. Leisen's skimmed over it lightly; his concerns are with the character of Death and his struggle for understanding, and with the love between Death and a girl who comes to discover who he is.

Fredric March and Evelyn Venable (who never had so rich a part again) played the strange lovers with an overwhelming sincerity; Leisen devised some breathtaking camera movements; the special effects used for March's various appearances were tactfully unsensational; and the whole delicate structure, which one false step could have wrecked, survives harmonious and intact. *Death Takes a Holiday* is forgotten now, but of all thirties films, this is the one that most demands revival.

Far left: Warner Oland and Henry Hull in **The Werewolf of London,** directed by Stuart Walker in 1935. Among the less familiar of Universal's essays in horror, **Werewolf** was quite an engaging fantasy. Oland, better known as Charlie Chan, played an Oriental werewolf, here seen grappling with Hull, the titular creature, an unfortunate English botanist whose condition was the result of a strange encounter in Tibet.

Below: Four suspicious scientists sharing a work-bench. In **Doctor X** (1932) they had separate labs, but here the publicity photographer managed to group them together. They were played by (l. to r.) Harry Beresford, John Wray, Arthur Edmund Carewe and Preston Foster. One of them had to be the strangler, so it seemed that one-armed Foster could be ruled out. Yet guilty he was – synthetic flesh had done the trick. Lionel Atwill presided over the establishment and Lee Tracy's reporter solved the mystery. The heroine was Fay Wray, testing her nerves for next year's encounter with King Kong.

The Great Comedians

Chapter 5

Comedy as the twenties had known it was rudely shaken by the arrival of sound. The three great comedians, Charles Chaplin, Buster Keaton and Harold Lloyd, went down different paths. Chaplin, reluctant to compromise, released two films only in this period, *City Lights* (1931) and *Modern Times* (1936). *City Lights* is a silent film with score and sound effects and is Chaplin's richest work; not so much a comedy as a gentle romance with supremely funny comic interludes, it matches him, for perhaps the only time, with an actress who in her own right could have carried a film, the lovely and gentle Virginia Cherrill (whom Chaplin at one point dropped from the film, before realizing the enormity of his error), and it shows that the silent film could have lived on happily, side by side with sound, if only others too had had the courage to persist.

Modern Times, still speechless apart from announcements and a nonsense song, marks the last appearance of Chaplin's little tramp, and closes a distinguished chapter of history. Inventive as its best passages are, there is a kind of tiredness about the film, a feeling that the moment has arrived when it is time to move on. In the forties Chaplin tackled new, exciting and surprising tasks.

Re-scaling the heights

Harold Lloyd did not hesitate to use the spoken word, but his voice proved flat and solemn, and the "regular fellow" of his great silents lost most of its sparkle as he grew older. Lloyd worked on, with five thirties features to his name, but his character was firmly rooted in the twenties scene, and only when he went back to the purely visual comedy of the climbing sequence in *Feet First* (1930) or the adventure of the moving tent in *Professor Beware* (1938) did something of the old zest come through.

Buster Keaton in the thirties was the saddest of figures. He had already lost his battle with MGM to retain complete control of his films; now personal problems hastened his decline. Until 1933 the studio still starred him in features, but good slapstick stuff though they were, anyone could have done them as well as Keaton did, and he sank to two-reel shorts and cameo appearances. The only genuine Keaton film of the thirties, *Le Roi des Champs-Elysées* (1934), was made in France. Far ahead, however, lay recovery, and a fuller recognition of Keaton's genius than the twenties had known.

The one silent comedian to relish and gain immeasurably by the coming of sound was W.C. Fields. That unmelodious, grating drawl added the last perfect touch to Fields's character – the rancorous, self-centered and self-deluding loner at odds with family, society and the world. Fields's thirties comedies never missed. In one year alone, 1934, he had three of his greatest successes: *The Old Fashioned Way*, a delicious period piece in the course of which Fields gleefully booted the obnoxious Baby LeRoy out of the room; *Mrs Wiggs of the*

*Cary Grant and Irene Dunne in Leo McCarey's **The Awful Truth** (1937). McCarey won the Best Director Oscar for the film.*

Below: *Harpo Marx and friend in **Animal Crackers** (1930). This was the Brothers' second film, made cheaply – and somewhat shoddily – at Paramount's Eastern studio at Astoria, Long Island. It was really just an appetizing hint of glories to come.*

Main picture: *Charles Chaplin and Virginia Cherrill in **City Lights** (1931). Chaplin spent three years and two months on this, his masterpiece. The scene shown here, the Tramp's first meeting with the blind flower girl, proved the hardest of all to complete, takes and retakes going on for months. The result was ample reward.*

Far right: *Chico and Groucho Marx in some devious skulduggery in **Monkey Business** (1931), the team's first Hollywood film.*

Cabbage Patch, when he appeared for the last half hour to enjoy the cooking of ZaSu Pitts ("More meat," he demands, with the air of a man just glimpsing paradise); and his masterpiece, *It's a Gift.* There have been few darker comedies than this. Fields's tribulations are even more painful than usual (the opening sequence as he vainly seeks sleep on his balcony is almost sadistic), and his relations with his dreadful family more fraught; the final escape to the orange grove in California seems merely to promise a temporary release. In *It's a Gift* a great clown touched the edge of tragedy.

Brothers in anarchy

The Marx Brothers at their best contrived a perfect blending of silent and sound techniques. Their first five films, from *The Cocoanuts* (1929) to *Duck Soup* (1933) were made for Paramount. That these films were their best was once accepted as an article of faith. Certainly Groucho's outrageous dialogue is at its most uninhibited here, and Harpo's visual punning and disordered logic attain a surreal intensity, but, and especially at the beginning, the production values were shoddy, Chico's function as an almost sane bridge between Groucho and Harpo is not fully developed and there is always poor Zeppo trying to justify his existence with a bland song or some half-hearted love-making. *Duck Soup* is far better than the other Paramount movies for it has a first-rate comedy director, Leo McCarey, and a less ramshackle plot.

The Brothers' move to MGM may not have promised well, but it came off splendidly. *A Night at the Opera* (1935) and *A Day at the Races* (1937), both directed by Sam Wood, are filled to the brim with joyous invention. Production is lavish, plots strong; Chico has some of the finest moments, and rises to them, and Allan Jones acts and sings a great deal better than Zeppo. Most of the cherished Marx memories come from these two films. *Opera* has the crowded cabin, the discussion over the contract, and the football game across the opera house, with the orchestra conned into a spirited rendering of "Take Me Out to the Ball Game". *Races* has Chico selling Groucho the form books and the breeding guides, Chico and Harpo and their ice-cream stall, and Groucho dumping his watch in the water ("Better rusty than missing"). It was all downhill after that, but the boys had done enough.

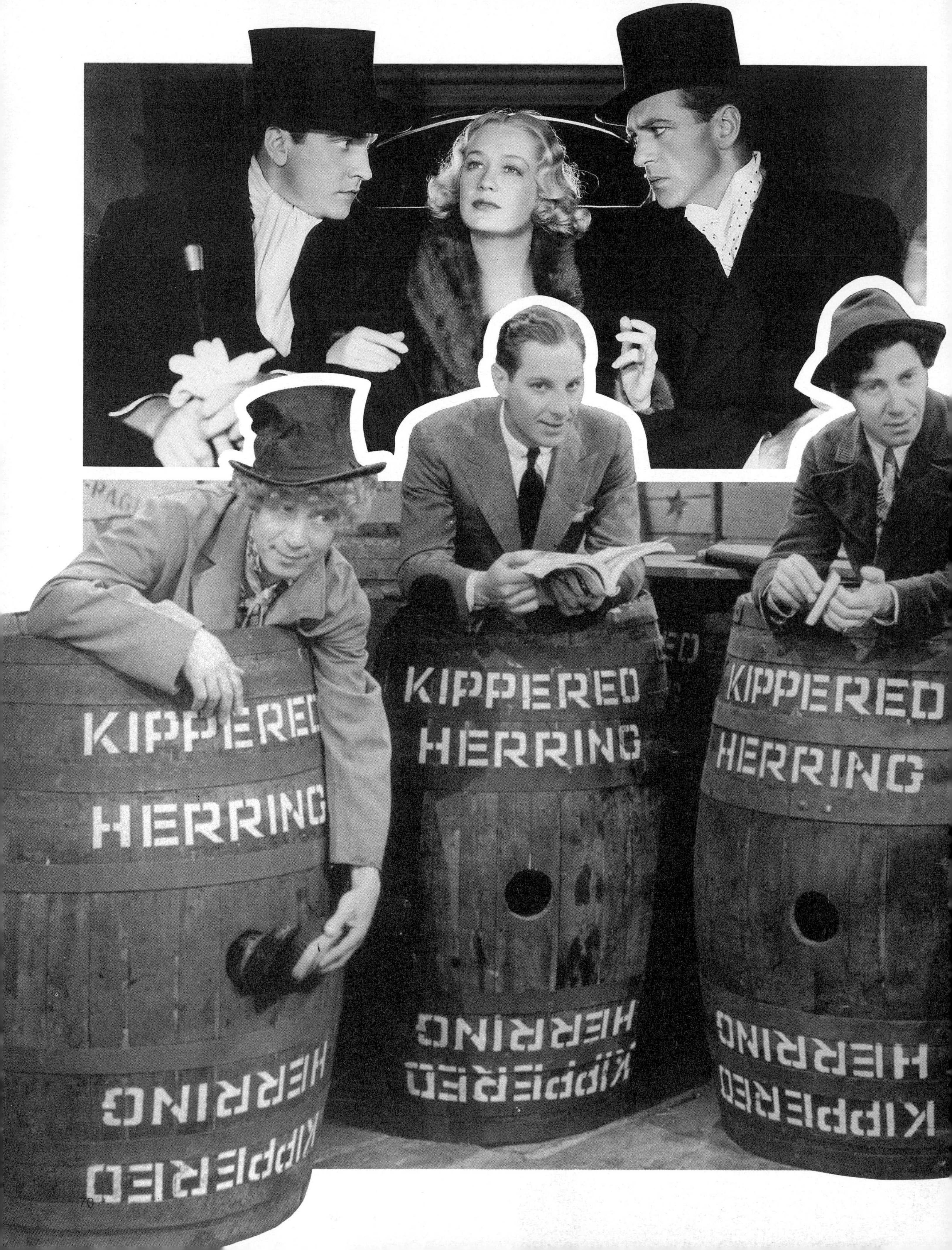
KIPPERED
HERRING
KIPPERED
HERRING
KIPPERED
HERRING

Main picture: *The stowaways and their hiding place. Harpo, Zeppo, Chico and Groucho in* **Monkey Business** *(1931).*

Left: *Fredric March, Miriam Hopkins and Gary Cooper in Ernst Lubitsch's* **Design for Living** *(1933).*

Below: *ZaSu Pitts, Jimmy Butler and W. C. Fields in* **Mrs Wiggs of the Cabbage Patch** *(1934). Fields is doomed to disappointment. He thinks Pitts is a magnificent cook, and marries her, little realizing that his meals arrive via a grinning Jimmy Butler.*

Memories of the comedies that Joe E. Brown made for Warners are much fainter – not Brown's fault, for these movies have rarely been revived. One at least should come back, the baseball farce *Alibi Ike* (1935). This has a story by Ring Lardner and a frenzied energy. Brown was a master of mugging and of comic timing, and it is sad that he should now be known simply for his occasional ventures, brilliant as they were, into prestige productions in supporting roles. The amorous millionaire of *Some Like It Hot* (1959) had been a star in his own right once.

These were the comedians, but there were other kinds of thirties comedy in which the comedians did not appear. In the polished, sophisticated comedy of manners the thirties excelled. They had much to build on, for the twenties had seen Chaplin (in *A Woman of Paris,* 1923), Lubitsch (in *The Marriage Circle* and *Lady Windermere's Fan,* 1925) and others raise the form to a delicate precision that the harsh intrusion of sound may have seemed to threaten. But Lubitsch himself, with *Trouble in Paradise* (1932), was there to show the way, and this delectable, entirely amoral comedy of two charming jewel thieves (Herbert Marshall and Miriam Hopkins) and their equally charming victim (Kay Francis) was an unflawed joy.

Marshall was cast too often as a stiffly respectable type, but here he showed an engaging lightness of touch; Hopkins was always twice the actress with this director than with anyone else, and the supremely ladylike Francis brought an ironic edge to all her poised elegance. This was a comedy of deceptive appearances, and Lubitsch makes the point succinctly in his opening shot. A Venetian gondolier sings romantically, and the camera cuts away to show that his gondola is a garbage scow. A lovely running gag makes the same point, with Edward Everett Horton, who has glimpsed Marshall at work, meeting him again and again, each time making desperate attempts to recall where he saw him before. *Design for Living* (1933) also paired Hopkins and Horton, but Noel Coward's play was intractable material, and although scenarist Ben Hecht claimed that one line only of Coward's survived, even Lubitsch couldn't turn it into cinema, despite a cast including Gary Cooper and Fredric March.

"Capra-corn"

Frank Capra gave the romantic comedy a different outlook. Lubitsch's characters would have caught the eye anywhere; Capra's could have lived next door, except that some of them were rather rich. His first thirties hit, *Platinum Blonde* (1931), is a familiar tale of an honest reporter dazzled for a while by a rich girl but coming back in the end to fellow-journalist Loretta Young. The rich girl is played by a young and uncertain Jean Harlow; the reporter by Robert Williams, a gifted leading man who died tragically young. Capra showed that he had learned to undercut the flippancy with a feeling for genuine emotion that was never forced or sentimental.

The ending of *Platinum Blonde* is essential Capra. Williams is consoling Young, who had thought she had lost him: "There, there, Gallagher," he says, "there, there." A trite enough line, but the way it is delivered makes you remember it for ever.

Capra's *It Happened One Night* (1934) is more famous and more familiar. Reporter and rich girl again, with ebullient Claudette Colbert, Clark Gable perfect as the tough, sceptical reporter, and one of the thirties' sublime character players, the querulous, choleric Walter Connolly, as Colbert's much abused father. The wayward adventure fairly bounced along, with the people encountered on the way an unfailing delight. Roscoe Karns was at his most hollowly ingratiating as a traveling man trying his charm on Colbert, with Ward Bond as a hot-tempered bus-driver coming a close second. The film swept up numerous Oscars.

In *You Can't Take It with You* (1938) Capra's eccentrics leave the margins to fill the screen. This is a fairytale of a feckless household with Lionel Barrymore at its head and accumulating a lifetime of unpaid tax demands. Spring Byington churns out unactable plays, Ann Miller practises ballet under the tuition of Mischa Auer, Donald Meek meets Barrymore by chance and moves in to make toys, and the ultra-dignified Halliwell Hobbes makes fireworks in the basement. And Jean Arthur is the one sane member, captivating the audience every bit as much as rich James Stewart.

Master of screwball

Preston Sturges directed some of the forties' most sparkling comedies, but in the thirties he was a scriptwriter, and in *Easy Living* (1937) provides director Mitchell Leisen with the material for one of those movies that in such days of wealth seemed like just one of countless carefree pleasures; on re-viewing now it amazes with its pace, control and featherlight daintiness of touch. Tycoon Edward

Left: *Jean Harlow in one of her first starring roles in Frank Capra's* **Platinum Blonde** *(1931).*

Two contrasting shots from **You Can't Take it With You** *(1938).* **Inset far left** *Ann Miller displays her balletic skills, rich visitor James Stewart is amused and sister Jean Arthur beams with pride. Meanwhile,* **below,** *Scottish character actor Donald Meek poses for a publicity shot. Somewhere along the line the ape bit the dust; there is no trace of him in the finished film. Nervous little Meek contributed richly to many a thirties film;* **Stagecoach** *(1939) and* **Young Mr Lincoln** *(1939) perhaps contained the finest Meek cameos.*

This page: *Alice Brady as hostess and Mischa Auer as simian guest, in Universal's* **My Man Godfrey** *(1936). After a brilliant stage career and some silent films, Alice Brady in the thirties was a versatile character player. She won an Oscar for* **In Old Chicago** *in 1938, and in her last film,* **Young Mr Lincoln** *in 1939, was outstanding as the accused boy's mother.*

Far right: *Carole Lombard, Roscoe Karns (above), John Barrymore and Walter Connolly in Howard Hawks' **Twentieth Century** (1934). Thinking that Barrymore is dying, Lombard at last signs a theatrical contract. Connolly and Karns, driven to distraction by the temperamental duo, envisage peace at last*

Arnold hurls a fur coat from a high window. It falls on working girl Jean Arthur – how many of the great comedies revolved round that fair head, wide eyes and husky voice? – setting up a delightfully complicated chain of events. At one point Arthur is shown into, and presented with, a luxury hotel suite. She looks at all the opulence without a word. Left alone, she sinks down and breathes "Golly!"

Comedies like *Easy Living* began as comedies of character, but often shaded off into the kind of zany farce that was called "crazy" or "screwball" comedy at the time. Gregory La Cava was a notable practitioner in this line, with *The Half Naked Truth* (1932) and *My Man Godfrey* (1936). The first of these, a ribald and unashamed riot set in Manhattan theaterland, has Lee Tracy in his non-stop-talking act as a press agent, flustered Frank Morgan as an impresario blackmailed by Tracy – who arranges for compromising photographs of Morgan and the luscious Lupe Velez to crop up in all kinds of surprising places – and the morose and massive Eugene Pallette as Tracy's assistant,

who, in a running gag worthy of Lubitsch, everyone in the movie comes to believe is a eunuch. *My Man Godfrey* sends scatterbrained rich girl Carole Lombard on a treasure hunt. Her treasure is William Powell, a gentleman down-and-out whom Lombard finds sleeping rough and introduces to her household as a butler. The debonair Powell straightens the family out in no time – what with a manic Mischa Auer prone to sit on the mantelpiece imitating an ape, it needed doing.

Carole Lombard had already shown that she was a great comic actress in Howard Hawks's *Twentieth Century* (1934). This astonishing film, which bewildered its first audiences by the sheer extravagance of its invention, is an abiding masterpiece. John Barrymore plays Oscar Jaffe, theater producer and egomaniac, who grooms Lombard to stardom, has her run out on him for Hollywood, finds her again in Chicago, and in the course of the journey back to New York on the Twentieth Century express, traps her into a return. Hawks let loose wispy little Etienne Girardot as a gentle lunatic plastering the train with religious stickers, spluttering Herman Bing as a fugitive from the Oberammergau Passion Play, Karns and Connolly as Barrymore's tormented entourage. Barrymore makes his penniless getaway from Chicago disguised as a Southern colonel, seizes on the Passion Play idea to offer Lombard the role of Mary Magdalen – she is not impressed – and has her back in the end, slavishly treading the chalk lines he draws on the stage floor, a puppet on the master's strings.

Grant and Hepburn

Hawks's other great thirties comedy, *Bringing Up Baby* (1938), presents a different kind of clash of temperament. Cary Grant is sane, if that is the word for a palaeontologist spending years reconstituting a brontosaurus; Katharine Hepburn the sweet madcap who changes his life. The comedy is serious enough at heart – what happens to Grant's ordered existence is frightening if you stand back to think – but the decorations are an irresistible distraction. Hepburn was at her peak at that time, and Grant approaching his. The way that they struck sparks off one another was something that actors managed with Hawks better than with anyone else. All Hawks's films were really about companionship. Sheer happiness sounds dull; Hawks saw things differently.

Nothing Sacred, directed by William A. Wellman in 1937, was the most mordant comedy of the period. Beautifully shot in the new three-strip Technicolor – which at that time was much brighter and sharper-edged than the subdued naturalism of later color – it has Lombard, wonderfully fey and vulnerable as a girl from Vermont who is believed (mistakenly) to be dying of radium poisoning, Fredric March as the reporter who takes her to town for a last fling and milks the story for every drop of fake emotion, and Charles Winninger as the country doctor whose wrong diagnosis causes all the trouble. Winninger is a man with a low opinion of journalists. "The hand of God," he fumes, "reaching down into the mire, couldn't elevate one of them to the depths of degradation." The film was a savage onslaught that should have made audiences ashamed to read a tabloid again.

But the age had its quieter comedies. Leo McCarey's *Ruggles of Red Gap* (1935) was among the best of them. Charles Laughton was perfectly cast as the suave English butler marooned in the mid-West as the result of a bet his master has made with roughneck Charles Ruggles. Roland Young, master of underplaying and the ideal foil to Laughton, is the master in question, ZaSu Pitts and Mary Boland flutter happily around, and the film comes to a splendid climax, using Laughton's superb delivery to marvelous effect, when the actor quietens and conquers the locals with his recital of Lincoln's Gettysburg Address. It took all the thirties' arrogance to believe they could get away with that. And of course they did.

*A master must always live up to his butler's standards. In **Ruggles of Red Gap** (1935), Charles Laughton (left) indicates the need for further drastic measures, while Charles Ruggles makes the best of it. Laughton gave perhaps his finest screen performance in this film, the third of four versions of a perennial American favorite.*

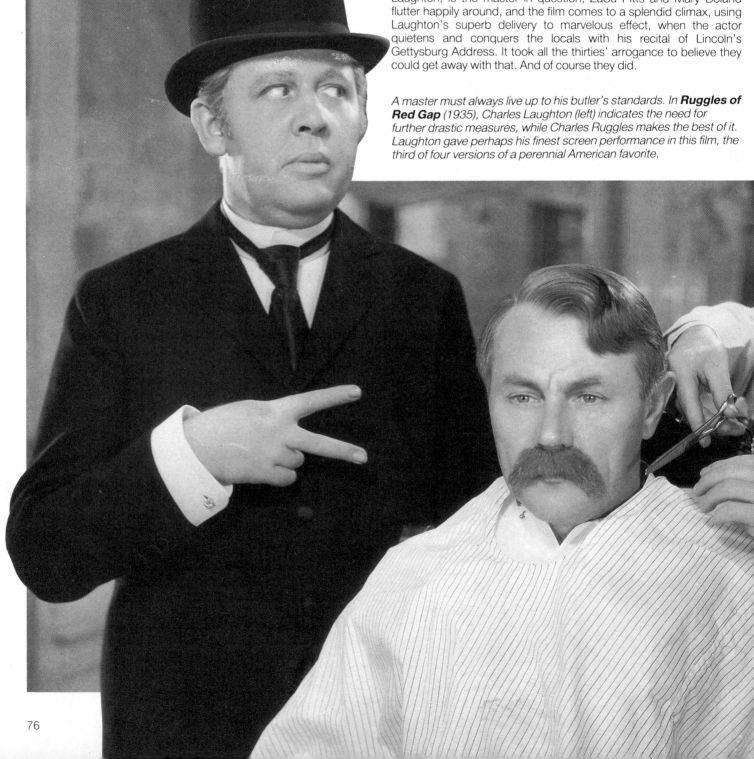

Above: *Clark Gable and Claudette Colbert urgently in need of a lift in* **It Happened One Night** *(1934). Colbert manages it, in one of the thirties' most fondly remembered scenes. The film collected all four major Oscars: Best Film, Best Director, Best Actor and Best Actress, a feat not matched until 1975.*

Below: *Cary Grant and Katharine Hepburn in the restaurant scene from* **Bringing Up Baby** *(1938). Hepburn's spectacular dress has suffered a revealing rip; Grant's embarrassment, and his efforts to cope, are a delight to watch.*

Main picture: *Will Rogers as steamboat captain and Berton Churchill as river-bank prophet in John Ford's* **Steamboat Round the Bend** *(1935).*
Below: *Humphrey Bogart is a one-man picket-line (aided by the dog) in* **Stand-in** *(1937). In a rare appearance in comedy, Bogart played Douglas Quintain, a producer driven to drink by his studio's troubles.*

Far right: **Ruggles of Red Gap,** *with the impeccable Charles Laughton a little under the influence. In the thirties players like Arthur Treacher and Robert Greig could make a living playing butlers: Laughton did it this once, and outshone them all. That fine comedian Edward Everett Horton had played Ruggles in the 1923 version, directed by James Cruze.*

This CAFE
is UNFAIR
to QUINTAIN

This CAFE is
Unfair
to me too.

Crackerbarrel philosopher

Will Rogers, vaudeville star, wry philosopher, and incarnation of the common man, died in an air crash in 1935. Rogers had had limited success in silent films, but like Fields he was one to gain enormously from sound. He needed the soft burr of his voice, the anecdotes, the easy, unmalicious wit. The last three years of his life were the years of his finest films. Henry King's *State Fair* (1933) was by far the best of the three versions Fox made of the story, and one of the all-time charmers. King was a master of Americana, quietly recording the small pleasures and the passing sadness of a way of life that was passing too. This story of a country family's visit, prize pig in tow, to the fair was beautifully cast (Rogers and Louise Dresser as the parents, Janet Gaynor and Norman Foster as their children, Lew Ayres as Gaynor's suitor) and superbly shot by Hal Mohr.

After this Rogers made three films for another director who loved the feel of the small American town – John Ford. *Dr Bull* (1933) was not strictly comedy – it was the story of a local doctor in Connecticut and his fight against an epidemic – but still revolved round Rogers' character, and his shrewd humors kept breaking through. *Judge Priest* (1934) had him down in Kentucky playing the little judge Billy Priest in a film that Ford would later remake, with much the same themes and characters, as *The Sun Shines Bright* (1953). Star and director showed an uncanny affinity, and in 1935 their last film together, *Steamboat Round the Bend*, was in its own right a

masterpiece. Rogers sells his medicine show to buy an old Mississippi steamboat, installs a wax museum, shelters a swamp girl touchingly played by Anne Shirley, and finally, in a sustained comedy sequence involving burning waxworks and patent medicines alike to squeeze out the last ounce of steam, discovers the missing witness, a vagrant prophet, who can save his nephew from a hanging. While *Steamboat* was being shot, Fox merged with Twentieth Century, and Ford claimed that the new management, eager to make an impression, cut out most of his comedy. But directors are not always the best guides to their own work, and one may well feel that the film's balance of comedy, drama and peaceful contemplation is just about right.

And there were others. Alfred E. Green's *The Dark Horse* (1932) was only a B-movie that rolled off the Warners production line, but it was that rarity, a political comedy. Publicist Warren William's attempts to promote an honest but entirely stupid Guy Kibbee for Governor ("Every time he opens his mouth he subtracts from the total sum of human knowledge") provided an hour of devious skulduggery and biting wit. Green also made *Baby Face* (1934), in which Barbara Stanwyck goes from rags to riches by offering her favors, rising floor by floor, to what seemed half the personnel of an enormous bank. Viewed seriously, this was a trashy melodrama; taken as a very dark comedy, which Green's camera rising gently up the bank's façade suggested it should be, it was a malevolent joy.

Below: *Irene Dunne and Melvyn Douglas in Richard Boleslawski's* **Theodora Goes Wild** *(1936). This was one of the first of the screwball comedies which were immensely popular in the later thirties.* **Bottom:** *Jean Harlow is unimpressed by Lee Tracy's latest piece of artwork in* **Bombshell** *(1933). Victor Fleming directed with enormous verve.* **Right:** *Constance Bennett and Roland Young in* **Topper** *(1937). Bennett and Cary Grant played ghosts who can only reach Heaven if they can point to a good deed; the deed is teaching Young, as Topper, how to enjoy life.* **Far right:** *Spencer Tracy in* **Libeled Lady,** *directed by Jack Conway in 1936. An heiress sued a newspaper for five million dollars; MGM deserved to make as much with this brilliant comedy.*

That's showbiz

The show-business comedy was usually musical, but it could be straight, when it liked to draw its fun from temperamental stars. Two such were Leslie Howard and Bette Davis in Archie L. Mayo's *It's Love I'm After* (1937). They played a quarrelling stage team, long engaged but frightened of the plunge, who took their feelings onstage with them, peppering their rendering of *Romeo and Juliet* with sotto – and not so sotto – voce insults. With Eric Blore always in attendance to stoke up the fires, this one was a brilliantly sustained comic tour de force, and Howard must have enjoyed it a great deal more than he had the year before, when he played Romeo in earnest in MGM's staid middle-aged romance.

In *Stand In* (1937) the movie business poked fun at itself. Leslie Howard's vein of studious puzzlement was just right for the role of Atterbury Dodd, a New York efficiency expert sent to examine the workings of an ailing studio. Aided by Joan Blondell as a stand-in who becomes his secretary, Howard routs the crooked tycoons, rescues producer Humphrey Bogart from the bottle, and puts the studio on its feet, with Bogart ensuring the success of its latest opus by cutting glamor girl Marla Shelton out of the movie and restructuring it round a gorilla. Blondell was her perky, delightful self, but Shelton had the film's great moment, helplessly drunk and sliding so, so slowly under the table during a vital discussion.

But the classic film of Hollywood self-mockery was *Bombshell* (1933). Jean Harlow, two years on from *Platinum Blonde* and now a polished performer, plays a star who has to endure the full blast of the studio's publicity machine, Lee Tracy runs that machine with a ruthless fury, and the movie never loses a chance to bite the hand that feeds it. In a beautiful piece of plotting, a group of aristocrats with whom Harlow is involved turn out to be hard-up actors hired by Tracy, and the most aristocratic of them all, dear old C. Aubrey Smith, is caught lamenting that back at the studio Lewis Stone gets all the good old man parts.

The Rough Side of Life

Chapter 6

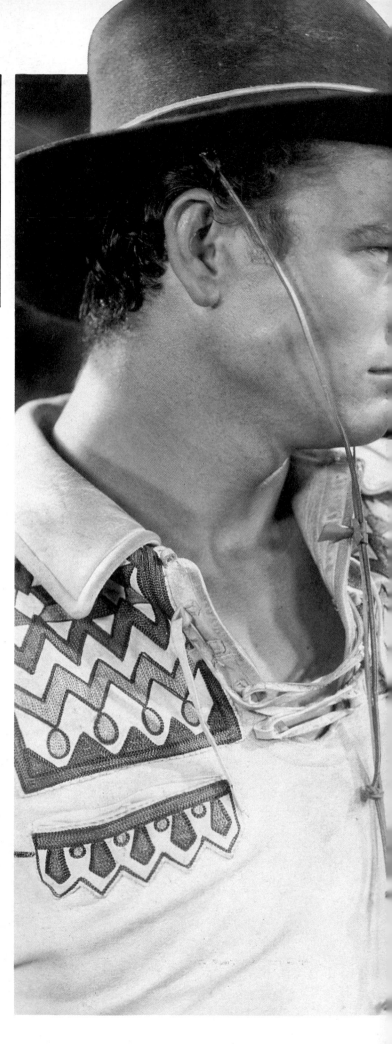

One of the cinema's great staples, the Western, was hardly prominent in the thirties. At the beginning, perhaps, that was not surprising. Difficulties of sound recording in the open took time to surmount; studios wanted to exploit the spoken word, and the cowboy was seldom a loquacious man. But as early as 1930 two directors, Raoul Walsh with *The Big Trail* and King Vidor with *Billy the Kid*, showed that it could be done. Walsh's film was in *The Covered Wagon* tradition, an episodic, spectacular production about the pioneers on the Oregon trail. It starred a very young, very raw John Wayne, who went on to a long apprenticeship in B-Westerns before his career took off with *Stagecoach* in 1939. Vidor's film, too, if not among his best, was a workmanlike job, steadily unsentimental, but a shade hampered by the uncharismatic John Mack Brown and Wallace Beery (and incidentally, one of the first films to be shown, in suitable theaters, in 70mm wide format, an innovation too expensive at that time to follow up).

But curiously, that was virtually that. Although minor Westerns were made in abundance, there was only one considered to be of any real importance, Cecil B. De Mille's *The Plainsman* (1936), between the beginning and the end of the decade.

A pacifist masterpiece

The war film was also infrequent in the thirties, but those that did emerge were uncommonly good. Lewis Milestone's *All Quiet on the Western Front* (1930) seemed to be one of the great ones in its time, and the years have taken nothing from it. For all the horror of its setting, *All Quiet* was a film of restraint, its most moving moments isolated from the mindless turmoil around. The idyllic pause with the French girls, the scenes of Lew Ayres's leave with his mother in Berlin, the off-duty scenes of the soldiers unsentimentally talking of war and peace, Ayres with the dying French soldier in the shellhole, the butterfly and the quiet, unnoticed death, all these and more went to make a film of intense humanity and understanding. *All Quiet* was a film that dared to see a war from the enemy's point of view, and a film that said, uncompromisingly, that all war was hideous and wrong.

No thirties film saw war as heroic. *The Dawn Patrol* was made twice, by Howard Hawks in 1930 and by Edmund Goulding in 1938. *Hell's Angels*, directed by Howard Hughes, had taken the headlines and the public's fancy in 1930, but Hawks's far less spectacular film was infinitely better. It concentrated on the officers of one squadron, with Neil Hamilton as the commanding officer who has to sit and watch his flyers die. It was a film about professionalism, always one of Hawks's concerns, but also a film about the misery of waste, as gray and undramatic as the theme demanded. Goulding's version fell little short. Basil Rathbone was excellent in the Hamilton role, but Errol Flynn's stock portrayal of a jaunty devil-may-care was a little distant from the mood of the rest.

*John Wayne and Tyrone Power, Snr, in **The Big Trail** (1930). Wayne had played a few bit parts only when director Raoul Walsh gave him this first real chance.*

Left: *Jean Arthur as Calamity Jane in* **The Plainsman** *(1936). This was one of the decade's most curious pieces of casting, and in this publicity still Arthur doesn't look too happy about it. But her sheer professionalism won through.*

Main picture: *Wallace Beery and John Mack Brown in* **Billy The Kid.**

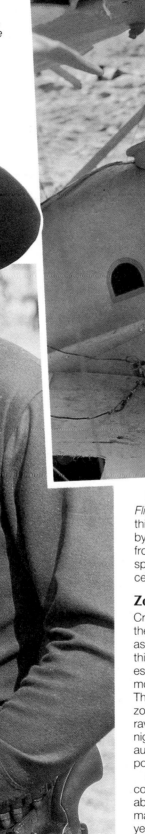

Not a war film but a film on the consequences of war was *The Last Flight* (1931). Another film that had to wait years for full recognition, this was the story of four flyers so damaged mentally and physically by the war that they cannot return home, staying in Paris and drifting from woman to woman, bar to bar. Not all survive. This was a film that spoke for a lost generation, a film that shunned pity as wholly as it did censure, preferring to watch and understand.

Zoo time

Crime, fantasy, musicals, comedy, Westerns, war films – these fit into their compartments easily enough. But one of the most striking aspects of the thirties was the sheer variety of the movies. The rest of this chapter is a random list of films that defy classification, but are an essential part of the decade's cinema history. Was there ever another movie, for instance, like Rowland V. Lee's *Zoo in Budapest* (1933)? The story takes place in one day, featuring a romance between zoo-keeper Gene Raymond and orphanage girl Loretta Young, ravishing photography from Lee Garmes, and a climax in the zoo at night with Young and Raymond, each a fugitive from an oppressive authority, being hunted down, and a frenzy of escaping animals pointing the moral that we are all prisoners until we break our bonds.

Another unique film was *The Power and the Glory* (1933). This consists of a series of intricate flashbacks with a probing commentary about the secret truths behind the life story of a great railroad magnate (Spencer Tracy). The film leaps back and forth across the years, the dead of one sequence are young again in the next, the narrator – the magnate's friend – sets moment against moment to build the whole sad mosaic of a life. Perhaps, after all, there was another movie like that. They made it eight years later, and called it *Citizen Kane*.

Every man's home...

The thirties had time, too, for the people at the bottom of the heap. The director Frank Borzage carried the unabashed lyricism of his silents across into the new medium in *A Man's Castle* (1933), where Spencer Tracy and Loretta Young are living through the Depression in a ruined shack on waste ground in New York, and *Little Man, What Now?* (1934) a love story set in depressed post-war Germany. There was no finer director of actresses than Borzage, and actresses like Janet Gaynor and Margaret Sullavan, who played some of their first and finest roles for him, carried over the loving serenity they had learned from him to their films for other directors. Sullavan was heart-breaking in *Little Man, What Now?* and no less so in Borzage's *Three Comrades* (1938), where his lovers are caught in the storms of rising Nazism in Germany. In *No Greater Glory* (1934) Borzage uses the battles of two gangs of street kids to make his anti-war moral; this was so powerful an indictment that some European countries, busily re-arming, took fright and banned it outright.

Another director, King Vidor, who had always shown sympathy with the small people of the world, made one of the most unexpected of Hollywood movies in *Our Daily Bread* (1934), the story of an agricultural co-operative in the New Deal's early days, and a film that brought to its climax – the irrigation of the hard-won land – an urgent and passionate joy. In these films Hollywood was far indeed from the dream factory of legend.

Borzage and Vidor were film-makers carried by the sheer force of their commitment. At another pole stood William Wyler, a craftsman who strained his players' patience with take after take until he had the result he wanted, but a craftsman of taste and intelligence, too. His *Dead End* has been discussed already. That was a filmed play, beautifully opened up for cinema, and the filmed play was Wyler's specialty. He turned Elmer Rice's *Counsellor-at-Law* (1933), the story of a high-powered attorney who comes to the verge of disbarment and suicide, into a compact and energetic film, with a towering performance from John Barrymore and a touching one from Bebe Daniels. In *These Three* (1936), a version of Lillian Hellman's play *The Children's Hour*, Wyler scored a notable victory over the censors and their code. The play had dealt with a supposed lesbian relationship between two teachers, as did the second film version in 1962, also directed by Wyler. In 1936, this had to go. Substituting a heterosexual triangle, Wyler left the play's charge – the destructive effects of scandal-mongering – intact, drew a portrait of a malevolent child (Bonita Granville) that had a lethal intensity, and gave Miriam Hopkins, the thirties' most underrated actress, the part of her career as the odd-girl-out of the triangle.

For *Dodsworth* (1936) Wyler turned to a novel by Sinclair Lewis. It was a film of quiet character-building, marvelously played by Walter Huston as the retired motor-manufacturer whose trip to Europe changes his life, by Ruth Chatterton, startlingly honest as the selfish and unfaithful wife, and by Mary Astor as the tranquil woman to whom Dodsworth turns. The last passage of the film, with Huston coming back across the bay to an Astor who thinks she has lost him, had a sudden surge of emotion that caught one by the throat, especially as it came from a director normally so unassertive.

Far left: *Wallace Beery, as Pat Garrett, confronts John Mack Brown in* **Billy The Kid** *(1930).*

Below: *Lew Ayres in* **All Quiet on the Western Front** *(1930). Perhaps in part through his involvement in this pacifist masterpiece, Ayres himself became a conscientious objector in World War II. Here he prepares to defend his shelter. A moment later he stabs a French soldier, and through the night has to watch him die. The Frenchman was played by silent comedian Raymond Griffith.*

Main picture: *Loretta Young in **Zoo in Budapest** (1933). The shot gives an idea of the visual splendor of this astonishing film.*

Left: *Helen Chandler, Walter Byron and Richard Barthelmess in **The Last Flight** (1931). This film, apart from a few German-language versions of other men's work, was the American début of German director William Dieterle, the man who, along with Michael Curtiz, set the pattern for Warners in the thirties.*

Right: *David Niven, Michael Brooke and Errol Flynn in the 1938 remake of **The Dawn Patrol.** This was a rare light-hearted moment in a film that, like the Hawks' original, looked at the war in the air with pity and pain.*

Headline material

Other thirties films of distinction stemmed from the stage. Lewis Milestone's *The Front Page* (1931) was from a play by Ben Hecht and Charles MacArthur, refilmed later by both Howard Hawks and Billy Wilder. Hawks and Wilder refashioned the piece to suit their own concerns, and gloriously so. Milestone left it relatively undisturbed, while doing justice to its savage cynicism and cut-throat wit. This was a newspaper film that made *Five Star Final* look benevolent.

Stage Door (1937) was from a play by Edna Ferber and George S. Kaufman, but arrived on the screen much rewritten, and almost certainly improved, by Morrie Ryskind, Anthony Veiller of *Winterset* and director Gregory LaCava. It tells the story of a group of actresses in a theatrical boarding house, has scathing dialogue (the sharpest darts delivered by Ginger Rogers and Eve Arden), a glowing performance from Katharine Hepburn as a society girl fighting for stage success, with a final speech, when she gets there, whose every intonation still echoes in the mind ("the calla lilies are in bloom again – such a strange flower..."), and a small part of a young, failed actress played by a newcomer, Andrea Leeds, with a dreaming, rapt intensity. Unhappily, Miss Leeds stayed in films for a short four years, had no other part that mattered, and retired to marry a millionaire.

Stage Door was the best film ever made about the theater. William A. Wellman's *A Star Is Born* (1937) did as much for the movies. This story had already been filmed by George Cukor in 1932 (as *What Price Hollywood?*), and Cukor would do it again in 1954 with Judy Garland, but Wellman's version was incomparably the best. With Janet Gaynor as the rising star, Fredric March as the setting one, Lionel Stander in his most venomous form as a brutal publicity man, and Adolphe Menjou all perplexed elegance as the studio chief, this was another superbly acted film, alive with memorable scenes – Gaynor's first meeting with March at the Hollywood Bowl, Stander's callous attack on March at the race-track, and the heartbreaking closing scene when, with March dead, Gaynor faces the crowds at her premiere ("This is Mrs Norman Maine...").

Giants at Fox

The Informer (1935) was also a remake, this time of Arthur Robison's neglected and excellent film of the same title, made in Britain in 1929. Robison was a German director, and Ford's film had a Germanic look about it, too, with its misty streets and flickering lamps, distorted camera angles and acting that verged on the Expressionistic. It had a tremendous central performance from Victor MacLaglen as the dull giant of a man who for a few pounds betrays his comrades (the film comes from Liam O'Flaherty's novel of the Civil War in Ireland), and a script from Dudley Nichols, who wrote *Stagecoach* and other films for Ford, that tinged the squalor and waste with a melancholy poetry.

This side of Ford, which it is now unfashionable to enjoy, had been there in late silents like *Four Sons* and *Hangman's House* (both 1928), and may have owed much to the fact that Ford was working then at Fox alongside the German master F.W. Murnau (*Four Sons*, in fact, uses sets from Murnau's triumphant *Sunrise*, made the year

Two scenes from **Dodsworth** *(1936).* **Far left:** *Ruth Chatterton, who had been a stage star for many years before beginning her short film career in the late twenties.* **Dodsworth** *was her last American film. She made two more in Britain, and then returned to the stage.*

Right: *Walter Huston and David Niven (right). Niven played one of Fran Dodsworth's numerous admirers; Ruth Chatterton's brilliant performance made the woman fascinating and appalling at once.*

Main picture: *Douglass Montgomery and Margaret Sullavan in* **Little Man, What Now?** *(1934).*

Above: *Edward G. Robinson and Boris Karloff in* **Five Star Final**
*(1931). Editor Robinson is sending failed clergyman Karloff to dig out
more dirt about a murder. The result was two suicides, a family
ruined, and a chastened Robinson quitting the tabloids. Crusading
films could put an end to a social evil, but this one was here to stay.*

Far right: *Ginger Rogers, Adolphe Menjou and Katharine Hepburn in
Gregory La Cava's* **Stage Door** *(1937). A marvelous example of
ensemble playing, the film was a perfect demonstration of the
strength of the studio system. There were at least a dozen superb
parts in this film, and as many more rewarding small ones. The actors
were there, all RKO had to do was fit them in. Note the elegant
contrasts of the décor, the work of Van Nest Polglase.*

before). Murnau died in a motor accident in 1931, but he had made two films that just fall into the thirties, and showed his powers intact. *City Girl* (1930) was a lyrical romance set in the Oregon wheatfields. Conceived and made by Murnau as a silent film, it suffered indignities at the hands of a studio prepared to make any sacrifice on the altar of sound. *City Girl* was recut, reshot, had comedy added, dialogue superimposed, all by other hands, and after all that, was little shown. The film lay in the vaults for forty years, reappeared in the seventies, with some intrusions removed, and was a revelation. Murnau's feel for wide open spaces, the gentle radiance of his lighting, his way of making a small, private drama into something as timeless as myth: these remained.

Murnau left Fox, set up a partnership with Robert Flaherty, and sailed for the South Seas to make his last film, *Tabu* (1931). Nominally a collaboration, the film is far more Murnau than Flaherty, the documentarist submerged beneath the poet. Still in 1931 a silent film, save for some natural sound and a voice raised here and there in song, *Tabu* was a dance of light and shadow, sunshine and bright water and quiet nights. The actors were natives who had never appeared before a camera, and the story was a simple, sad one, of two lovers parted by the curse of "tabu", of renunciation and a tragic end. Murnau had no time for cinema's eternal South Seas theme of happy islanders corrupted by the white man and his ways. His islanders played their story in their own world and on their own terms. *Tabu* was a thirties masterpiece – and the last, proud defiance of the silent film.

Starburst

Chapter 7

No one, back in the thirties, had yet coined the word "megastar", but the phenomenon was there just the same. MGM, of course, led the way with their slogan "More stars than there are in heaven", and those stars included Greta Garbo and Clark Gable, William Powell and Myrna Loy, Joan Crawford, Norma Shearer, Robert Montgomery and a host of others now among the all-time greats.

The divine Garbo

Effortlessly, Garbo dominated them all. She was not only the finest actress of her time; she was one of the most fortunate. Through all of her American career she made no film away from MGM, and the reward of that loyalty was that she had the best the studio could offer – the best in sets and costumes, a variety of serviceable stories, the camerawork of William Daniels, the direction of Clarence Brown, who made five of her thirties films, and of such fine stylists as Edmund Goulding, George Fitzmaurice, and Rouben Mamoulian. Garbo was always herself, serene, secret, lit from within, but screen acting has always been about being oneself. The camera is a merciless critic of mere impersonation; the great screen actor offers a series of variations on the self, and manages to inhabit those variations with an unshaken belief.

Garbo made 13 films in the decade; they were part of a continuing autobiography. In *Anna Christie* (1930) she speaks for the first time, giving Eugene O'Neill's sad waif her own dignity and pride. *As You Desire Me* (1932) sees her essaying Pirandello, matching his mysteries with her own, and granted a worthy partner in Erich von Stroheim. For *Queen Christina* (1933) she insisted that her old partner John Gilbert, now facing a ruined career, play opposite her. Gilbert justified her faith; the old gaiety returned, a new maturity with it, and he seemed set to re-establish himself. Unhappily Gilbert's personal troubles persisted, and he made only one more film before his death in 1936. With *Anna Karenina* (1935), *Camille* (1936), and *Conquest* (1937), Garbo had three triumphs in a row. Of three very good films the last was perhaps the best, a beautifully mounted and really convincing historical film. She was marvelous as Marie Walewska, Napoleon's Polish love; Charles Boyer was an energetic and extremely human Napoleon; and Maria Ouspenskaya was in terrific form as an old lady who will stand no nonsense from this upstart Frenchman. He has to play cards with her, like a good boy.

The magic of Marlene

Over at Paramount, Marlene Dietrich reigned. Of her first seven American films, six were directed by Josef von Sternberg, whose film *Der Blaue Engel* (*The Blue Angel*, 1930), made in Germany, had

*Greta Garbo and Ramon Novarro in George Fitzmaurice's **Mata Hari** (1932). This was their only film together, and in it Garbo as the glamorous spy performed what* Variety *magazine described as "a polite cooch to Oriental music". But she performed it with pride.*

transformed Dietrich from an actress little known outside her own country into an international star. Seldom have the careers of a star and a director been so closely interwoven. Sternberg's genius was for the pictorial; a master of lighting, as well as of design, he filled his movies with one harmonious, richly decorated composition after another, with the focal point always his star. A lesser actress might have become part of Sternberg's set, as lovely and as lavishly adorned as the rest, living but null. But with Dietrich it was not so. Her personality, mocking, arrogant and sensual, needed to be tamed by Sternberg's delicate artifice, just as his eternal perfectionism cried out for the warmth of his star.

Of their films together, two are masterpieces. *Shanghai Express* (1932) is one of those films where the sheer mastery of the opening sequence (in this case the train weaving its slow way through the crowded chaos of a Chinese town) makes one certain that everything will go well. Quoted and caricatured a hundred times, Dietrich's Shanghai Lily is still a fantastic creation, striking fire from the buttoned-up Englishness of Clive Brook, and making exotic Anna May Wong seem in comparison a mundane little thing. Yet *The Scarlet Empress* (1934), where Dietrich plays Catherine the Great, is even better, with the star marvelously extending her range to embrace the shy girl of the beginning, the passionate empress of the central love affair, and the triumphant Amazon of the climax, riding her white horse up the palace stairway as music, camera and set seem to blend and dissolve into one exultant whirl of delight.

What Katy did next

This was too heady a brew for its first audiences, and the film made very little money. Neither did many of the movies that another great star, Katharine Hepburn, made for RKO. Hepburn at that time just did not fit the popular image of a film star. Strikingly beautiful she was, but her voice was high-pitched, cultured and sharp, her eyes agleam with intelligence. This one was too much her own woman to capture her audiences' affection. In the end, of course, she did, but not until the forties, the move to MGM, and the partnership with Spencer Tracy. Yet to those who did warm to her, the young Hepburn's thirties films were a succession of surprising pleasures. At another studio she might have been groomed into a semblance of convention. At RKO, the studio's weakness for the wayward, and even bizarre, was the very thing needed to engage her formidable talent.

Hepburn's range was astonishing. In *Morning Glory* (1933) she was herself, an ambitious young actress aquiver with high ideals; in *Spitfire* (1934) she became a hoydenish mountain girl; in *Alice Adams* (1935) she was a small town girl with intellectual pretensions; while in *Sylvia Scarlett* (1934) she became a fairground nomad, most of the time disguised as a boy: four different women, yet once again, four variations on a single theme. There was *Stage Door*, too, and *Bringing up Baby*, *Mary of Scotland* (1936), a romanticized account lent conviction by Hepburn's radiant queen, and, on loan to Columbia, *Holiday* (1938). Here she rejoins Cary Grant to play the eccentric daughter of a stuffy family, taking refuge in her room and the company of her two low friends, caustic Jean Dixon and Edward Everett Horton at his bumbling best. It adds up to a wonderful decade for Hepburn, despite the poor box-office, and she entered the forties with one of her best films, *The Philadelphia Story* (1940).

Right: *All that director von Sternberg and Paramount had made of the incomparable Marlene Dietrich went by the board when she crossed to MGM for the musical* **Kismet** *(1944), once described as "a musical looking for a score". Dietrich not only had to endure this outrageous costume; her name was billed below the title for the first time in her Hollywood career.*

Far right: *Katharine Hepburn in* **Christopher Strong** *(1933), directed by Dorothy Arzner. A superior soap-opera, this movie had Hepburn as an aviatrix who deliberately crashes her plane and kills herself because she loves a married man who cannot bear to leave his wife. Arzner was a talented director, but only* **Nana** *(1934) and* **Craig's Wife** *(1936) gave her real chances.*

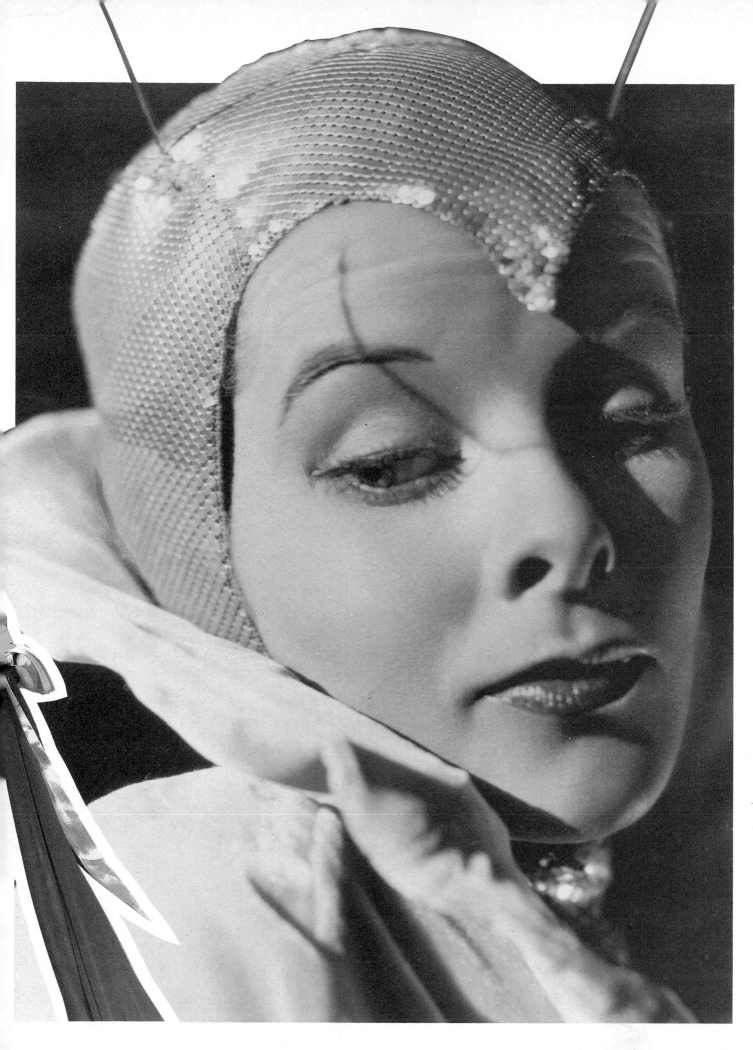

Ladies in waiting

Garbo, Dietrich, Hepburn – these three had the star quality, the presence, that is as unmistakable as it is impossible to define. But others shone brightly too, if not as intensely, and sometimes not as long. Darkly beautiful and elegant, the patrician Kay Francis was immensely popular in the early thirties, proving that audiences didn't mind your being a lady so long as you weren't intellectual with it. Before Dietrich established herself, Francis was Paramount's leading star, and lucky in her films, with *Ladies' Man* (1931), *Cynara* (1932) and *Trouble in Paradise*, and when she moved to Warners in 1932 she gave her finest performance, in *One Way Passage* (1932). The story of a shipboard romance between a dying woman and a man returning to be executed for murder (William Powell), this should have been mawkish rubbish, but the quality of the playing, the tactful script, and director Tay Garnett's cool refusal to linger on sentiment, make it a triumph. And the movie said it all in just 69 minutes – it was a different world.

Another elegant lady was Norma Shearer, who in 1927 had married Irving Thalberg, MGM's wonder boy and supervisor of production until his death in 1936. This was no unmixed blessing for Shearer. In silent days she had been a charming and witty soubrette; now, with Thalberg behind her, she could pick her parts, and too often picked them in the studio's most prestigious, and dullest, efforts. But she was perfectly cast as Elizabeth Barrett in *The Barretts of Wimpole Street* (1934), acted with a touching restraint, and convinced one that she might have written the poetry (as Fredric March's boisterous Browning singularly did not).

Also at MGM was Joan Crawford, whose urgent portrayals of ambitious working girls were worthy of rather better films. For Crawford, the directors and stories she needed lay ahead. In the thirties, only the occasional *Grand Hotel* (1932) or *The Women* (1939) rose above the routine affairs to which the studio consigned her.

The stars whose forte was sophisticated comedy fared much better, for here the thirties could do no wrong. Claudette Colbert was not everyone's Cleopatra (in the 1934 version), but her effervescence and her irresistible smile carried her happily through almost everything else. Carole Lombard, once Paramount realized her gift for comedy, was fey, scatter-brained and adorable, and after *Twentieth Century* never looked back, while Jean Arthur had the same warmth and sense of fun as Lombard, and a full measure of shrewd realism as well. And by the time the thirties ended, other reputations were being made. Rosalind Russell was developing from the ultra-refinement of her early roles into a comedienne with poise, a way with a line and a ferocious attack; the young Judy Garland was making her way; Ginger Rogers was striking out, without Astaire, as a comedy star in her own right; and Bette Davis at last had the dramatic roles for which she had fought so long. The forties would bring yet more.

Right: *Kay Francis and William Powell in* **One Way Passage** *(1932). They were a popular team, with seven films together in the early thirties. They matched each other in elegance, sophistication and for quality acting.*

Below: *Rosalind Russell, Joan Fontaine and Norma Shearer in George Cukor's* **The Women** *(1939). Russell stole the film with an all-out display of predatory, self-centered bitchiness.*

Left: *Ronald Colman and Madeleine Carroll in* **The Prisoner of Zenda** *(1937). The high adventure and high romance of Anthony Hope's much filmed tale were perfectly suited to Colman, but director John Cromwell fared less well. The film was made for independent producer David Selznick, who had additional scenes shot by WS Van Dyke and George Cukor without even consulting Cromwell, fine as Cromwell's work on the film had been. It had to be to keep up with his predecessors; Edwin S. Porter, George Loane Tucker and the great Rex Ingram had made the three previous versions.* **Above:** *Douglas Fairbanks Junior, and Colman in the same film. Fairbanks was Rupert of Hentzau, a part which made Novarro a star in 1922.*

The perfect gentleman

In the twenties Rudolph Valentino, Ramon Novarro and Ronald Colman had been the greatest stars. Now the sex balance was shifting. Valentino was dead, Novarro and Gilbert in decline, and no man's popularity rivalled that of Garbo or Dietrich. Yet Ronald Colman was a survivor. The romantic hero supreme of silents like *Stella Dallas* (1925) and *Beau Geste* (1926), Colman continued playing leads for another twenty years, his mellifluous voice making him even more effective with sound. Sometimes, with Colman, time seemed to stand still. *The Prisoner of Zenda* (1937) was the remake of a silent film, and had the same uncomplicated morality, the same unassuming charm. Colman was adept at suggesting a kind of raffish nobility. His Sydney Carton in *A Tale of Two Cities* (1935) and his François Villon in *If I Were King* (1938) were perfect examples of this, but his occasional forays into the modern world, as in John Ford's *Arrowsmith* (1931), gave the impression that he had seen it all so many times before, and the result was not so convincing.

King Gable

Through the thirties, Clark Gable was the king of MGM. In his first years at the studio there was a touch of the heavy about Gable, and in retrospect these films seem to be his best. His first great hit was in *A Free Soul* (1931), where as a gangster he came near to taking the film away from Shearer and Leslie Howard. He played opposite Garbo in *Susan Lenox: Her Fall and Rise* (1931), and was at his tough and swaggering best with Jean Harlow in the steamy jungle passions of *Red Dust* (1932). As Gable's popularity grew, the studio made his parts more sympathetic, and he lost something of his fire; sometimes, too, he was sadly miscast, in *Idiot's Delight*, for example, and *Parnell* (1937). A little ahead, however, lurked *Gone with the Wind*.

John Barrymore in the thirties was not the star he had been. Now in his fifties, his health broken by alcoholism, he was often dependent upon a cue-board for his lines. Yet Barrymore was the supreme professional, and none of his troubles, save perhaps at the very end, was visible upon the screen. The list of his thirties performances is as impressive as that of his glory days in the silent films; to the old panache he added a sad sense of fatality that fairly wrenched one's sympathies. In one scene from *Grand Hotel* he outacts Garbo (the first, and the only, time); in *A Bill of Divorcement* (1932) he plays father to the young Hepburn, a father just back in the world after years in an asylum, and gave her her first glimpse of what great screen acting could be; and in *Romeo and Juliet* (1936) his Mercutio, though

inevitably far too old, blazes gloriously, and for a while makes that misjudged venture take on a semblance of life.

Barrymore emerged late in his career as a great comedian. First there was *Twentieth Century*; then *True Confession* (1937), where he was with Lombard again, playing a character who was sometimes agreeably eccentric, sometimes unnervingly deranged; he ran away with the film, leaving you wondering whether perhaps it wasn't comedy at all. His last triumph was in *Midnight* (1939). Here he plays a French count, serenely unflappable, concerned only to save his wife (Mary Astor) from the consequences of a foolish affair, who at one point (in one of the thirties' sublime moments) finds himself compelled, in his bedroom in Paris, to give a devastating impersonation, by telephone, of an ailing baby in Budapest. That was how far thirties comedy could go.

Above: *Carole Lombard and Gable starred in Paramount's* **No Man of Her Own** *in 1932. Here they are seen off duty during the filming. Gable and Lombard married in 1939. Three years later came the tragic air disaster in which she died.*

Left: *Clark Gable and Jean Harlow in* **Red Dust** *(1932). Mary Astor was the third member of this triangle drama set in the Malayan jungle. Twenty-one years later, the movie was remade as* **Mogambo**.

Below: *Margaret Sullavan and Robert Taylor in Frank Borzage's* **Three Comrades** *(1938). Taylor, Franchot Tone (outstanding) and Robert Young played the three friends caught up in the social and political turmoil of post-war Germany; Sullavan was the girl who married Taylor and died of consumption. The script, with its romantic insistence that friendship and love could lightly conquer death, provided a rare screen credit for Scott Fitzgerald, who adapted Erich Maria Remarque's novel.*

Right: *Clark Gable and Spencer Tracy in* **San Francisco***, one of the biggest hits of 1936. The climax, with the earthquake and fire of 1906, was a stunning sequence, with superb special effects by Arnold Gillespie. It ended with Jeanette MacDonald leading the survivors back from the hills into the now quiet city as the title song welled up. Nonsense, but wonderful.*

The MGM men

The personality of Spencer Tracy underwent an odd change in mid-career. Fox had seen him in the early thirties as a rough and rugged type. As soon as he moved to MGM in 1935 the image changed and the gentle, reliable, almost patriarchal Tracy was born. In *San Francisco* (1936) and *Boys' Town* (1938) he played priests, still ready to use his fists if necessary, true, but that total integrity was not as interesting as the old, flawed hero. He went on, inevitably, to great men of history, in *Edison the Man* (1940) and *Northwest Passage* (1940), but the forties saved him. The characters he played opposite Hepburn fused the two Tracys. The roughness came back, counter-pointing her elegance, and the honesty remained.

The climate of the later thirties worked a similar change in the character of James Cagney, and as the decade went on, it became apparent that smoothness, even suavity, was the quality a male star must have. There had always been a cultured poise about Herbert Marshall, William Powell and Adolphe Menjou, but now, and particularly at MGM, there came the day of the man about town. That studio alone had Powell, Robert Montgomery, Franchot Tone, Robert Taylor, Robert Young and Melvyn Douglas. The quality of their material varied, but these, too, were professionals, and their work made the tritest story watchable. And they could all rise to a better opportunity, as did Tone and Young in *Three Comrades*, Douglas in *Tell No Tales* (1939), Taylor with Garbo in *Camille*, Powell in the Thin Man series and *My Man Godfrey* (1936). Montgomery would not have a real chance until later on, with *They Were Expendable* (1945).

More than mere charm

Finally, a reputation that would steadily grow through the thirties and beyond – that of Cary Grant. Grant began at Paramount in 1932, soon appeared opposite Dietrich in *Blonde Venus* (1932), and twice with Mae West, in *She Done Him Wrong* (1933) and *I'm No Angel* (1933). That was competition indeed. Ramshackle affairs though her movies were, Mae West swept through them like a force of nature, joyously mocking her own sexuality, and Grant perforce, as he had done with Dietrich, stayed quietly on the sidelines. But these films led to better things for him. He went on to RKO and Columbia, specializing at first in crazy comedy, and one of cinema's great actors made his presence felt. Superficially, Grant belonged to the man-about-town brigade, but behind the casual charm and the easy confidence a much more complex character was barely hidden. *Bringing up Baby* (1938) is as moving as it is, for all the comic trappings, precisely because it is so clear that Grant's work matters very much and that he cannot lightly surrender to the Hepburn world. Later still, that side of Grant could take on a darker tinge, and he became the perfect ambivalent hero for Alfred Hitchcock. And it is in his thirties films – *Bringing up Baby*, *Holiday*, and above all *Only Angels Have Wings* (1939) – that the outlines of his Hitchcock heroes can be traced.

Above: *Cary Grant and Irene Dunne, with Ralph Bellamy (**right**), in Leo McCarey's **The Awful Truth**, made at Columbia in 1937. One of the biggest box-office hits of the year, it was a sophisticated screwball comedy which had Grant and Dunne as a young couple who divorce and contest access right to their dog. They get together at the end of the film, of course – the remarriage theme being fairly common to the genre (see also **His Girl Friday,** 1940; **The Philadelphia Story,** 1940; **Woman of the Year,** 1942; **Adam's Rib,** 1949), but enacted only after the couple has gone through a period of learning. The dog? He was played by Asta, William Powell and Myrna Loy's wire-hair terrier co-star in the 'Thin Man' films.*

1939
The End of
an Era

Chapter 8

The thirties had begun with the Depression. They ended with war in Europe, but they ended in cinema with such an outpouring of riches, in that one year of 1939, as had not been seen before – nor would ever be again. This was not an American phenomenon alone. In the Soviet Union, Alexander Dovzhenko made *Shors*; in Britain, there was the young Carol Reed's *The Stars Look Down*; in France two complete masterpieces in Marcel Carné's *Le Jour Se Lève* and Jean Renoir's *La Règle du Jeu*. As for America, there had been one miraculous year before, 1927, the year of Murnau's *Sunrise*, Vidor's *The Crowd*, Borzage's *Seventh Heaven*, Sternberg's *Underworld* and Paul Leni's *The Cat and the Canary*. But even 1927 could not boast the sheer number and variety of great films made in 1939.

Ford out West

Even since 1917, John Ford had produced great works from time to time, and in between had done his best as a studio pro, but now Ford made three films in the year; two of them were magnificent, and the third not far behind. Ford's contribution to 1939 was *Stagecoach, Young Mr Lincoln*, and *Drums along the Mohawk*. (Next year he added *The Grapes of Wrath* and *The Long Voyage Home* – no director ever made five films of such stature in so short a time.) *Stagecoach* rescued the Western from obscurity, and John Wayne from the B-movie grind. Ford went to Monument Valley, to become with the years his personal preserve, and brought back a movie perfectly shaped and timed, a movie that progressed, with not one dead or irrelevant frame, from the quiet intimations of trouble in the opening scenes to the shattering double climax of the Indian attack and the shoot-out at Lordsburg, and had still up its sleeve the most delicate and joyful of codas. And it was a film of great character performances too, with Thomas Mitchell, Donald Meek, Andy Devine, all of them down to Chris-Pin Martin's frightened little Mexican, supporting the central duo of Wayne and the marvelous Claire Trevor with their varied, idiosyncratic, unassertive skills.

With *Young Mr Lincoln* Ford was returning to a subject he had treated in *The Prisoner of Shark Island* (1936). That film had begun by rivalling D.W. Griffith with a masterly handling of Lincoln's assassination, had followed this with a harrowing sequence of the execution of the conspirators, and then tailed off somewhat as it traced the story of Dr Mudd, the man who tended John Wilkes Booth. Now there was no faltering. Taking its hero only as far as his election to Congress, *Young Mr Lincoln* was at once an affectionate picture of small-town

*Claudette Colbert arrives in Paris in the opening scene of **Midnight** (1939). One group of cameramen shot exteriors and background at the real Gare de l'Est; Paramount duplicated the carriage interior back at the studio, with hard wooden seats constrasting beautifully with the gold lamé gown.*

life and a reflection on greatness in the making, and it drew from Henry Fonda, in the first of his seven films with Ford, the definitive portrait of utter integrity. Fonda had been in films for four years, always competent, never quite imposing himself. Now the Fonda character was molded, and would endure for forty years.

Drums along the Mohawk, set in the Revolutionary War period, was Ford's first film in color, and if not the equal of its two predecessors, was still a film with a great deal to admire. There was Claudette Colbert, spirited as ever as a young bride coming to live in the Mohawk Valley, and only briefly disconcerted by finding Chief Big Tree standing silently in her kitchen; Edna May Oliver defying the world from her great bed; the melancholy return of a defeated army; and a marvellous final scene, with Fonda pursued by Indians across fields and forest, in which Ford used shades of color superbly to convey an emerging and brooding mystery.

Garbo laughs!

Ernst Lubitsch went to MGM to make his only film with Garbo. The result was one of the decade's finest comedies, *Ninotchka*. Garbo was the Soviet envoy captivated by Paris, a pretty hat and capitalist idler Melvyn Douglas – by the Lubitsch world, in fact – and the shrewd comic sense she revealed did not lessen the warmth of feeling that was hers alone. There were nicely varied characters in the three officials whom she is sent to check on, explosive Sig Rumann, wistful Felix Bressart, and dour Alexander Granach; a touching cameo from old Richard Carle as Douglas's servant whom Garbo wants to free from serfdom ("Go to bed, little father"); that memorable scene in the workmen's cafe when Garbo fails to see the cream-in-your-coffee joke before being convulsed by a simple pratfall; and so much more. Lubitsch gave the whole film a happy glow, scoring points off East and West alike, and in his response to Garbo finding a deeper humanity than he had shown before.

Mr Smith Goes to Washington, Frank Capra's contribution to 1939, was naive enough as a political tract, and its story of a country boy triumphing over the hard hearts and cynical moralities of Washington invited a total disbelief. But it was Capra's privilege to see the world in those terms if he chose, and his skill with actors was never more evident. This time he had Claude Rains (as a silkily devious senator) and Thomas Mitchell, Edward Arnold and Eugene Pallette, and with Jean Arthur doing her best to help the country boy prevail, and James Stewart as the shy idealist hero, there was a built-in guarantee.

John Ford's
three triumphs of 1939.
Far left: *Jessie Ralph, Ward
Bond, Henry Fonda and Claudette
Colbert in* **Drums Along the Mohawk.** *One
of Ford's great strengths was his use of the same
actors in film after film; the rock-solid yet sensitive Bond was
a vital member of that stock company.* **Top:** *Henry Fonda in* **Young
Mr Lincoln.** *The young lawyer broods on the future, and on the world
far away from Springfield.* **Above:** *John Carradine, Louise Platt and
John Wayne in* **Stagecoach.** *Carradine, another Ford regular, played a
courtly Southern gambler; Platt was the wife on her way to join her cavalry officer
husband, and bearing her child en route: Wayne as the Ringo Kid is out for revenge.*

Left: *James Stewart makes his marathon speech to the Senate in* **Mr Smith Goes to Washington** *(1939). The book is the Standing Rules of the Senate. Jean Arthur has just signaled from the gallery that he should turn to Rule 5, Section 3. On doing so he recalls all Senators who have walked out on him, so outsmarting the professionals.*

Below: *Marlene Dietrich in* **Destry Rides Again** *(1939). Her condition is the result of that famous fight with Una Merkel.*

Right: *James Stewart and Dietrich in the same film. Neither had appeared in a Western before. Stewart would go on to many more, Dietrich to only one. That is Fritz Lang's* **Rancho Notorious** *(1952), where her femme fatale was a typical Dietrich role.*

Stewart's career ran parallel to Fonda's in many ways. They began in the same year, 1935, reached the top at the same time, projected the same image of unassuming decency – and each did some of his best work for John Ford. Stewart's roles were varied in his first years – and he was even the murderer in *After the Thin Man* (1936). The Stewart character could be distraught, tentative or ill at ease, but perseverance was the keynote, pleasantness the weapon that disarmed. Though he made many Westerns later, it was a surprise to find him in one in 1939, and an even greater surprise to find Marlene Dietrich leaving her silks and satins to join him there. The movie was George Marshall's *Destry Rides Again*, an old Tom Mix vehicle dusted off and given lashings of comedy (Mischa Auer was a lugubrious Russian out West), catchy ballads, a hero who disapproved of gunplay and, to make up for that, a scratching, kicking, hair-pulling battle between Dietrich and Una Merkel. Those who had found Sternberg too rarefied warmed to Dietrich in this one.

In George Cukor's *The Women* battling ladies were the whole film. A ruthless parade of sharp-clawed scandalmongering, *The Women* gave glorious chances to Rosalind Russell as the most lethal-tongued of them all, to Joan Crawford as a home-breaking, hard-as-nails shopgirl, and to Norma Shearer as the nice woman who is the victim of it all. And Paulette Goddard, away from her work with Chaplin, scored as a spunky chorine.

Angels with Dirty Faces, the year before, had brought back the gangster film, and now Warners followed up with Raoul Walsh's *The Roaring Twenties*. A leading director since 1915, with a notable record in the twenties, Walsh had faded of late, but with this one he was right back on form. Again the film found an ingenious way of retaining the gangster as hero. An authentic-seeming prohibition period piece, it presented James Cagney as a basically decent man who comes back from the war, loses his job, and drifts into the rackets, but redeems himself by a noble self-sacrifice. The really evil character, played by Humphrey Bogart, still a supporting actor, is killed by Cagney. There was a documentary air about parts of the film, an interesting look ahead to the forties thrillers like *Boomerang* and *The Naked City* with their location shooting and realism.

Good Queen Bette

By 1939 Bette Davis was the unchallenged queen of Warners. She made four films for the studio that year. *The Private Lives of Elizabeth and Essex* has striking sets, and Michael Curtiz to whip it into life, but Errol Flynn, splendid as Robin Hood the year before, was a lightweight Essex, and Davis had to battle on alone. In Edmund Goulding's *The Old Maid*, a tactfully managed tearjerker, she has the strongest of competition from Miriam Hopkins, and profits by it, and in William Dieterle's *Juarez* plays the unbalanced Empress Carlotta, making a relatively small part, if a showy one, really crackle with energy. By far the best of the four films, however, was Goulding's *Dark Victory*. Davis plays a selfish society girl who learns that she is suffering from a brain tumor, and within months will go blind, then die. She was perfectly cast, the petulance and tantrums of the early scenes slowly yielding to a serenity that was something entirely new in her work.

John Barrymore's tour de force in *Midnight* has been noted, but it was not the only delight in director Mitchell Leisen's finest film. Claudette Colbert is a dancer stranded in Paris, posing as a countess to enjoy the luxury of Barrymore's house for a few days; Don Ameche plays the cab-driver who loyally supports her (by far the best thing Ameche ever did); and the dazzling script is by Billy Wilder and his writing partner Charles Brackett. Although he had directed one film in France, Hollywood did not give Wilder the chance to direct until 1942. In 1939 he was flourishing as a writer. He and Brackett had (along with Walter Reisch) written *Ninotchka*, and *Midnight*, an oddly tender film behind airy badinage was a fit companion piece.

Far left: Bette Davis, who begun her illustrious film career in 1931 and by the end of the decade was recognized as one of Hollywood's greatest actresses; this studio portrait actually dates from 1943. **Left:** Davis as cockney waitress Mildred in John Cromwell's **Of Human Bondage** (1934). She made this film on loan from Warner Brothers to RKO, and it gave her one of her first important roles as a scheming woman. Her co-star, Leslie Howard, would reappear with her back at Warners in two films directed by Archie L. Mayo, **The Petrified Forest** (1936) and **It's Love I'm After** (1937). **Above:** Claudette Colbert and Don Ameche in Mitchell Leisen's **Midnight** (1939), an elegant, cynical screwball comedy that could have only come from one studio — Paramount.

115

Above: *Ray Bolger (Scarecrow), Judy Garland (Dorothy, carrying Toto) and Jack Haley (Tin Man) in* **The Wizard of Oz** *(1939). Bolger's film appearances were sporadic, and often in poorish films, but he was an unfailing pleasure. Haley's other films were unrewarding, but his gentle humor was perfect for this, his richest part.* **Far right:** *Vivien Leigh and Clark Gable in* **Gone With the Wind** *(1939). Gable's performance as Rhett Butler was the high point of his career. Effortlessly dominating every scene in which he appeared, he gave his parts of the film a force and directness, and a humanity, that were often lacking elsewhere. Vivien Leigh* **right:** *in the same film, wanders through crowds of Confederate wounded. This sequence, with its famous crane-shot, was the work of the gifted designer Cameron Menzies. Selznick wanted 2500 extras for the scene. 1500 were available: 1000 dummies made up.*

Over the rainbow

Some of the finest thirties films are seldom seen. Others, luckier, have had unending revivals, in repertory cinemas, on TV and video. MGM made one such in 1939 – *The Wizard of Oz*. No film is better known, or better loved, and *Wizard* deserves all its acclaim. It gives full scope to the rich and little used talents of Ray Bolger, Bert Lahr and Jack Haley as Dorothy's three companions, has the enchanting freshness of Judy Garland, some of the screen's best songs, and an overwhelming air of happiness. You feel that, once again, as they said it had been in the pioneer days, movie-making was fun. And *Wizard* teaches one lesson that a student of the thirties needs, that you don't have to believe the credits. The director of record is Victor Fleming, who did indeed make most of the film, and finely too, but the opening, sepia-toned sequences in Kansas and Garland's song of the Yellow Brick Road were the work of King Vidor.

Victor Fleming is credited, too, as the sole director of *Gone With the Wind*, the most famous film of 1939 – and of the whole decade. Again the credits lie. George Cukor directed a few scenes, Sam Wood and the art director William Cameron Menzies several more. The sheer scale of the film commands respect. Menzies' designs are outstanding, Margaret Mitchell might have written Rhett Butler for Gable (and probably did), Leslie Howard and Olivia de Havilland are perfectly cast, too, but a nagging doubt remains. Without the years of assiduous publicity, the worldwide search for Scarlett, would the film have made the impact it undeniably did? For *Gone With the Wind* is hollow at the core, partly because of producer David O. Selznick's numbing conviction that this trashy best-seller was a great novel, partly because Vivien Leigh's Scarlett is a posturing doll. The part cried out for Bette Davis; failing that, Carole Lombard could have schemed and charmed her way through, and mocked all the pretensions as she went.

Flying out in style

As *Gone with the Wind* went on its garlanded way, a simple action melodrama crept almost unnoticed through the cinemas. Made by Howard Hawks, it stars Cary Grant and Jean Arthur, Richard Barthelmess and Rita Hayworth, and is called *Only Angels Have Wings*. *Only Angels* is set in a South American port called Barranca, headquarters of a tiny airline whose pilots fly mail across the Andes. Grant is the chief pilot; Barthelmess a disgraced flier ending up in this God-forsaken place to escape, and work again; Hayworth his wife (and an old flame of Grant); Arthur an entertainer marooned there; Thomas Mitchell Grant's right-hand. A fine cast, and a routine story, it seems. But that is to forget Hawks. Hawks had made great comedies, but not yet a dramatic masterpiece, though in *Scarface* he had come near.

The great triumph of *Only Angels Have Wings* could not have been planned. It is far too easy and spontaneous for that. In every foot of the film there is a breathtaking sympathy between director and players. The tone is laconic, casual; two people die in the film, two people whom the audience has come to admire, yet still the mood is joyous and carefree. In *Love's Labour's Lost* there is the line to "move wild laughter in the throat of death", and that is precisely what *Only Angels* does. Joe (Noah Beery) dies, and Grant eats the steak that Beery has ordered. "Who's dead? Who's Joe?", he says to an uncomprehending Arthur, and before the film ends Arthur will understand in her turn. The Kid (Mitchell) is dying. He asks Grant what has happened. "Your neck's broken, Kid," says Grant, and Mitchell, taking a last puff at Grant's cigarette, understands too, not just the fact, but the weight of love behind the words.

The flying scenes in the film are thrilling enough, but many directors could have made them. In *Only Angels* it is the people that matter, and in that run-down building that is airport, hotel, restaurant and bar all in one, Hawks's characters learn, and teach each other, how to face the world outside, and survive. And in this hard-won optimism is the magic of the film. *Only Angels Have Wings* was the bravest of endings to the decade, and perhaps the greatest of American sound films.

So the thirties ended, and with them a world. The cinema would go on, but while thirties audiences still lived, the cinema as they had known it, a universal, popular art, was nearing an end. Yet how the thirties movies, the best of them, and at odd moments the worst of them, had soared. In the last analysis Howard Hawks was wrong. Not only angels had wings.

Cary Grant and Jean Arthur posing for the publicity still for **Only Angels Have Wings** *(1939). A perfect pairing in a perfect film. Grant and Arthur appeared together only twice (the other was* **The Talk of The Town** *in 1942), but they struck sparks from one another. In* **Only Angels** *Grant is worldly wise: Arthur thinks she is, but isn't. By the end she has come some way.*

Title Changes

British distributors changed the titles of many American films. Films mentioned in this book were retitled as follows:

U.S.		G.B.
The Black Cat (1934)	:	The House of Doom
Bombshell (1933)	:	Blonde Bombshell
Conquest (1937)	:	Marie Walewska
The Doorway to Hell (1930)	:	A Handful of Clouds
The Gay Divorcee (1934)	:	The Gay Divorce
Holiday (1938)	:	Free to Live
The Hollywood Revue of 1929	:	The Hollywood Revue
Mad Love (1935)	:	The Hands of Orlac
The Most Dangerous Game (1932)	:	The Hounds of Zaroff
Our Daily Bread (1934)	:	The Miracle of Life
The Power and the Glory (1933)	:	Power and Glory
The Public Enemy (1931)	:	Enemies of the Public
Underworld (1927)	:	Paying the Penalty
The Whole Town's Talking (1935)	:	Passport to Fame

PICTURE CREDITS